EVANGELISM NOW:

Cultivating Influence that matters

Evan Herrman

www.TotalPublishingAndMedia.com

Endorsements

"In this book, Evan Herrman gives us all a historical and a proactive look at evangelism. Within these pages, you will come to learn that evangelism is not only what you do, but who you are. This book will make a difference in your life today and throughout eternity."

**Jim Stovall,
bestselling author _The Ultimate Gift**

"In this book EVANGELISM NOW, you will learn how to cultivate influence that matters. Influence that impacts those around you. Based on your personality, you will learn to identify your unique gifts in evangelism, as well as ways to overcome obstacles which prevent you from living a life of practical evangelism. This book is one of the best for individuals and for the church."

Keven Sorbo

"In his new book EVANGELISM NOW, Evan Herrman provides a practical, yet engaging, resource for churches, pastors, and laypersons alike. Every ministry serious about reaching the lost needs this book!"

Lucas Miles
Pastor and Best Selling Author, Woke Jesus

Acknowledgments

I am grateful to God for all the inspiration and creativity, and for guiding me through the process of writing this book. His presence and inspiration have been the driving force behind every word penned on these pages.

To my incredible wife and family, your constant support and understanding have been my rock throughout this journey. Your unwavering belief in me and the work I do provide the foundation upon which this book stands. Your belief in me to keep pursuing ministry over many years has been such an encouragement. Your love and support is my greatest strength. This work is a reflection of the collective support and inspiration which has and still does surround me. Thank you all for being an integral part of this endeavor.

A heartfelt thank you goes out to the many mentors who have played pivotal roles in shaping my perspective and nurturing my growth. Your wisdom, guidance, and encouragement have been invaluable. You know who you are, and your impact on my life is immeasurable.

To every reader who embarks on this journey with me, thank you for joining in the exploration of the ideas and experiences shared in these pages. Your openness to the message of this book is a gift. I am truly grateful for your time and consideration.

In gratitude,
Evan Herrman

Foreword by Nick Vujicic

My Friend Evan,

As I sit down to write these words, I can't help but marvel at the incredible journey you've been on over the last few years with this book. From the highs to the challenging lows that tested your resilience, it has been a testament to the beauty that which emerges in the form of this book. You have embraced every moment of writing it with courage and with purpose.

Now, here we stand on the threshold of something extraordinary – the release of your first book, EVANGELISM NOW. From the very moment you shared your vision for this book I knew it was destined to be more than just a collection of words on pages. It is a call to action, an anthem of transformation, and a roadmap for those seeking to live a life infused with the spirit of God for his work in the world – by living a lifestyle of evangelism.

I've had the privilege of witnessing the dedication and sacrifice you poured into each chapter, each paragraph, and each sentence. Your commitment to excellence, coupled with your passion for souls, radiates from every page. And, Evan, I want you to know the impact of your labor of love will undoubtedly reach far beyond what you might imagine.

In the opening chapters, you explore the very essence of evangelism – the heartbeat of sharing the Good News. You delve into its evolution and styles and debunk myths that have hindered its understanding. It's a comprehensive journey that sets the foundation for what follows – a guide, a mentor, and a companion to those yearning to embrace a lifestyle of evangelism.

Your focus on the skills needed for effective evangelism, coupled with the courageous exploration of difficult conversations, demonstrates a wisdom beyond your years. The tactical insights on objection handling, the stories of lifestyle evangelism, and the deep dive into presence-based evangelism are testaments to the richness of your experiences and the wealth of knowledge you've gained.

Chapter by chapter, you unravel the intricate dance between the believer and the Holy Spirit, highlighting the divine partnership that breathes life into our efforts. The practical advice on building meaningful relationships and the courageous confrontation of fear, both from a biblical and neurological perspective, are needed in the church today. Your vulnerability in sharing your journey through fear, and your triumphs over it will undoubtedly resonate with every reader.

Evan, this book is more than a manual – it's an invitation. An invitation to live a life of influence, to become a lifestyle evangelist, and to build relationships that truly matter. It's a call to embrace the role of the Holy Spirit in our endeavors and to understand fear from a perspective that empowers rather than paralyzes.

As I reflect on the words you've penned, I am reminded of the transformational power of a life lived with purpose. Your words echo the sentiment that each of us, regardless of our circumstances can be a vessel of hope, love, and salvation. EVANGELISM NOW is not just a book; it's a movement waiting to unfold, and I am honored to stand beside you as it takes flight.

May every reader find within these pages not just a guide but a companion – a companion for their journey towards a life of soul-winning, a life that echoes the very heartbeat of Jesus, the greatest evangelist of all time.

With admiration and excitement for the lives that will be touched,

Nick Vujicic

Index

Introduction

Hey there,

I've been doing some thinking and reflecting, and it's led me to put pen to paper and share my thoughts with my brothers and sisters in Christ. Being a broken human being and Christian, I've come to realize a lot of us are sailing in the same boat – feeling like we might not be the best representatives of God. Having a sense of not being ready, of not having it all figured out, or what it takes to represent God here on earth. Being a good representative of God has gnawed at me for years. And, it's not just me; I see it echoed in churches and in the lives of believers all across the globe.

Now, I've taken up this writing task because I'm a firm believer Jesus is on His way back for His bride – that's us, the church. However here's the thing: we must be doing our part; sharing the good news with those around us. As Christians, we need to be out there genuinely spreading the word and effectively witnessing for Christ. Still, many feel they have not had proper training or guidance. So, that's where this book comes in – think of it as your guide to making a mark, making a difference in those areas of life that truly count. I have a personal conviction to love others back to life – to help people accept Jesus as their Lord and Savior.

See, here's the deal – God didn't just randomly create you and me. He's gifted us with this unique blend of talents and relationships, and they're not just for show. These talents are to play a crucial role in carrying out the great commission. And that's what I want to unpack here. Through these pages, we'll dive into what evangelism is all about. We'll check out different styles of evangelism, and here's the fun part – we'll try to match these styles with your gifting and personality traits. It's like finding the puzzle pieces that fit into your unique design – that best represents the image of Jesus.

But wait, I'm not just stopping at that. We're going to get real and dig into the good and not-so-good stuff about these personalities we've got. It's like a reality check – understanding where we shine and where we might need a little work. And oh boy, don't even get me started on the stories of the myths and misconceptions we seem to tell ourselves about being a witness for Christ. We will bust those myths wide open and set the record straight.

Practical? You bet. I'm not here to give you theories and leave you hanging. Nope, I've got your back. I will serve up topics to help you tackle the roadblocks folks often have regarding Christianity. We're going to break down those barriers one by one.

And you know what else? Rejection – that's a tough pill to swallow. I believe this book can help us heal from that hurt and conquer the fear of it. It's all part of living a life that counts, a life that has an impact, a life that's aligned with the great mission we've been given.

So, here's to taking that step toward understanding, influencing, and embracing the call of the great commission. This book is me learning as I go and sharing it with you as you walk that journey for yourself. My thoughts and experiences are woven into every word. Let's make our mark together, let's light up the path, and let's witness who we're meant to be.

God, I pray over this reader in Jesus' name that you will limit distractions as they are reading this book and use the lessons I have learned to spark new life into the reader's heart and mind. That through this process, fear or doubt about being a witness for you will go away, and the spirit of confidence and boldness will rest upon them in Jesus' name, Amen.

CHAPTER 1

Why does Evangelism means so much to me?

Have you ever been to a church camp? I was attending a camp called Drygulch. I was about seven years old and it was my first time. It was the last day of camp, and there was an altar call for kids who wanted to be in ministry to come forward for prayer. I felt like I had a profound thought at that moment, only to be followed by what a little kid's imagination could only be. I thought to myself, I do not want to be in ministry; most kids are on a spiritual high and only coming up because it's the last day of camp. Besides, I want to be a cop or a firefighter. I wanted to be a good guy. Halfway through that prayer, I heard God speak to my seven-year-old heart, **"That was supposed to be you up there."**

From that day forward, I have intensely desired to be in and do ministry. Because I did not understand the complexities of different ministry types, I wanted to be a pastor.

From that point on, my life was dedicated to becoming a pastor. I know, right? A seven-year-old dedicating his life to be something. But it's true. I was consistently spending time with God from a young age. I would carry my bible with me to school.

I would talk about Jesus everywhere I went. I never recognized that many of the gifts I was displaying were Evangelism. I often got made fun of, bullied, or, dare I even say, persecuted from the age of seven through high school for being a Christian and following "the rules." After graduating high school, I went on to college at Oral Roberts University. I got my degree in theology with a concentration in local church pastors. After graduation, it felt like I could not get a church job to save my life. I entered the workforce and had many jobs; how many you ask? I had twenty-one jobs before I got into real estate. I also had many part-time jobs during my time as a real estate agent. I landed a youth pastor job in 2015, and while I liked the youth, I did not have the gift to be a youth pastor. So that only lasted a year. I did not consider Evangelism as an option even though my life and gifts reflected Evangelism. I did not awaken to this idea of ministry until November 21, 2020, when I felt like the Lord gave me a vision, a word for Evangelism.

There was an event in 2013 that, now looking back, is when I believe the mantle of evangelist came upon my life. Like many of you, I have had a worst day of my life. This particular day was one of them. I remember as if it was yesterday. A Sunday afternoon, and my pregnant wife, who was halfway through her pregnancy, was having severe pain. I took my wife to the emergency room, and they sent us up to labor and delivery.

One of the nurse's first tests was using an ultrasound to find a heartbeat for the baby. The monitor was silent and motionless as the nurse was searching my wife's stomach for our child's heartbeat. At this moment, we started to get the deep, sickening feeling in our gut that life was about to go bad. We learned our daughter was no longer with us. All the plans, the dreams and future we were planning with and for her were stolen from us. Our hearts were broken, and we were sick.

After learning of the results of the test, it took another 24 hours for the stillbirth to take place. I had prepared myself for the birth of my stillborn daughter. We knew she was already gone. The grieving had started the day before. We knew what to expect through the process and had come to grips with the reality of her being gone. Before the birth, the Dr. gave my wife different painkillers so as not to experience the birth – it would help with the emotional aspect and keep her from being traumatized by the whole process. The hopes was she would not remember the physical pain which went with the emotional pain.

Because of this, my wife became tired coming off all the different medications. I was in the room mostly alone that day. We had visitors in and out, like my parents, In-laws, our pastor, and my best friend. But mostly, I felt alone. Nothing could have prepared me for what I would experience at seven-thirty that evening. I was sitting on that pink fake leather hospital couch holding my daughter when the nurse came into the room. After having and holding our daughter for seven hours, the nurse came in and said to Mr. Herrman it is now time for us to take her body. I had come to grips with her death, but I was not prepared for having to hand her body over, never to see or hold her again.

The amount of pain, desperation, and anxiety I felt was as if life itself was being sucked right out of me. Have you ever been swimming as a child and been held underwater to the point that you could not breathe and were desperate for oxygen? It felt like that but a million times worse. I could not breathe while desperately needing oxygen. And just like that, my daughter was gone. All that was left was dry heaving on an empty stomach and side pain till I could rehydrate my body with water after crying so much.

Fast forward a few hours, from seven-thirty to about nine at night. My wife is asleep again, and I am lying on the hospital couch. I did not blame God for us losing our daughter. I know that God is good no matter what. I knew God did not need another little angel in heaven, He did not take her from us. Her life was cut short because an enemy came to steal, kill, and destroy. Regardless, I still needed to see God's love in all that. So I say to God in my desperation, where is your love in all this? Because I don't see it and desperately need to see your love.

I immediately had a flashback to that moment at seven-thirty when I handed my daughter's body to the nurse. All that pain, desperation, and anxiety flooded back in and it felt as if life itself was being sucked right out of me. I said God, I asked to see your love; why did you show me this? I heard him say, "Evan, this is exactly how I feel when any of my children live a life without ever knowing my love." At that moment, I understood God's heart for those he called to be children but never accepted his love and salvation. I understood the pain of a father, having a child who never knew my love, as a hurt and broken father. I became a little more like God in a way I could have never imagined or understood. Because of this, I felt like I had become one with my Father in a way I had never experienced before.

I had many questions surrounding the loss of our daughter. I asked God why we even got pregnant in the first place. Why could we not have just skipped the pregnancy, and my wife never got pregnant? I heard God say, "Her eternal plan and purpose far outweighs any hurt, pain, or suffering you would feel." So, in amazement, I respond, what is her eternal plan and purpose? This was one of those slap-your-forehead moments because I realized I already knew the answer once God answered me. He said, "Her eternal plan and purpose is for her to dwell with me and for me to dwell with her. That is the same reason I created humans, knowing they would sin and knowing the eternal plan is for them to dwell with me and me to dwell with them. This far outweighs any hurt, pain, or suffering I go through to bring my children back to me."

This is why he was willing to send Jesus because the short-term hurt, pain, and suffering are nothing compared to the hurt of not knowing God and his love for our life. When we miss out on his love, it grieves the heart of God. So I made a promise that day, not to God but to Satan, that I would stand at the gates of hell and redirect traffic. So people would know the power and love of God and would experience his grace in their lives. Through this experience, salvation, and heaven became more real to me than I have ever experienced. I had to believe that eternal life with Christ and salvation is true, and that it is the most important thing on earth for people to experience. This story is why I am passionate about talking to others about Jesus. Because I know the hurt and pain of the Father if his children never know his love. God wants his creation to know his love, and it is our job as believers, to share that love with others so they can experience the love of the Father.

Evangelism has become a Christian word that many want to cringe at. It's only because we have made it that way. Next to experiencing the love and salvation of Jesus, the love of the Father, the second highest calling is to share that love with others. This is my experience and why I am so passionate about telling others Jesus loves them and motivating Christians to experience God's love in a way that leads them to share his love with others.

What is Evangelism and its evolution?

Evangelism is a term that has been used for many centuries. But what is its purpose? It is the act of intentionally spreading the Gospel, also known as the good news of Jesus Christ and his teachings to the world. People who do this by profession are called evangelists. But you don't have to do it for a living to be an evangelist. Evangelism is about sharing the message of Christ through our words and actions, which we are all called to do. Many Christians throughout history have been called evangelists. Still, many others don't hold the title of evangelist but are – they share the love of God with others in classrooms, offices, and work-places. They share the good news wherever they are.

There are three great examples of Jesus teaching us to go out and share the Gospel. The first public record is of Jesus sending his disciples two by two to other cities to minister to those in need. This work is unique because, by this point, this commission was part of their training. Even in their training, Jesus told them they have the ""authority to drive out impure spirits and to heal every disease and sickness." This is found in Matthew 10:1; Mark 6:7–13; Luke 9:1–2. This sending was with power and authority before they were even given the holy spirit. So we don't need to "feel the holy spirit" to go do ministry. While feeling the holy spirit is not required, it is good practice to learn how to live a life led by the spirit. The disciples were sent out without the indwelling of the holy spirit the first time out. You don't not need to feel the holy spirit to talk to people about Jesus or to do good works. I often notice I feel the spirit after I engaged in the conversation or the acts of service. Later the disciples were more prepared with the holy spirit to do the work of the great commission, because they had the indwelling of the holy spirit and learned to live life by the spirit.

The second time we see Jesus sending people out to do ministry is in Luke 10. The Sending of the Seventy-Two event demonstrates Jesus' strategy of reaching out to various towns and places to announce the imminent arrival of God's kingdom. It reflects the urgency and inclusivity of Jesus' message – it's not limited to just His immediate presence. This mission prefigures the broader mission of the early Church after Jesus' resurrection and ascension. In essence, the Sending of the Seventy-Two illustrates Jesus' desire to expand His message and prepare people's hearts to receive Him, showcasing His concern for the lost, and his disciples' participation in spreading the good news.

(NIV) Luke 10. **"**After this the Lord appointed seventy-two others and sent them two by two ahead of him to every town and place where he was about to go. **2** He told them, "The harvest is plentiful, but the workers are few. Ask the Lord of the harvest, therefore, to send out workers into his harvest field. **3** Go! I am sending you out like lambs among wolves. **4** Do not take a purse or bag or sandals; and do not greet anyone on the road. **5** ""When you enter a house, first say, ''Peace to this house." **6** If someone who promotes peace is there, your peace will rest on them; if not, it will return to you. **7** Stay there, eating and drinking whatever they give you, for the worker deserves his wages. Do not move around from house to house. **8** "When you enter a town and are welcomed, eat what is offered to you. **9** Heal the sick who are there and tell them, ''The kingdom of God has come near to you." **10** But when you enter a town and are not welcomed, go into its streets and say, **11** ''Even the dust of your town we wipe from our feet as a warning to you. Yet be sure of this: The kingdom of God has come near." **12** I tell you; it will be more bearable on that day for Sodom than for that town.**13** "Woe to you, Chorazin! Woe to you, Bethsaida! For if the miracles that were performed in you had been performed in Tyre and Sidon, they would have repented long ago, sitting in sackcloth and ashes.**14** But it will be more bearable for Tyre and Sidon at the judgment than for you. **15** And you, Capernaum, will you be lifted to the heavens? No, you will go down to Hades. **16** "Whoever listens to you listens to me; whoever rejects you rejects me; but whoever rejects me rejects him who sent me." **17** The seventy-two returned with joy and said, "Lord, even the demons submit to us in your name." **18** He replied, "I saw Satan fall like lightning from heaven. **19** I have given you authority to trample on snakes and scorpions and to overcome all the power of the enemy; nothing will harm you. **20** However, do not rejoice that the spirits submit to you, but rejoice that your names are written in heaven." **21** At that time, Jesus, full of joy through the Holy Spirit, said, "I praise you, Father, Lord of heaven and earth because you have hidden these things from the wise and learned and revealed them to little children. Yes, Father, for this is what you were pleased to do.**22** "All things have been committed to me by my Father. No one knows who the Son is except the Father and no one knows who the Father is except the Son and those to whom the Son chooses to reveal him." **23** Then he turned to his disciples and said privately, "Blessed are the eyes that see what you see. **24** For I tell you that many prophets and kings wanted to see what you see but did not see it, and to hear what you hear but did not hear it." Through this passage, we can find several meanings and lessons.

- **Cooperation and Teamwork:** Jesus sends out the disciples in pairs, emphasizing the importance of collaboration and mutual support in ministry.

- **Trust in God's Provision:** By sending them minimal supplies, Jesus teaches them to trust in God's provision rather than rely on their own resources.
- **Hospitality and Receptivity:** The instructions about peace and hospitality underscore the importance of receptivity and openness to God's message.
- **Response to Rejection:** Shaking off the dust was a symbolic action used to show that they've done their part, and the responsibility now falls on the ones who rejected the message. Lastly, we recognize the purpose of Jesus preaching about and calling all towards great commission.

Matthew 28:16-20 (NIV) **16**. "he eleven disciples went to Galilee, to the mountain where Jesus had told them to go.**17**. When they saw him, they worshiped him, but some doubted. **18**. Then Jesus came to them and said, "All authority in heaven and on earth has been given to me. **19**. Therefore go and make disciples of all nations, baptizing them in the name of the Father, Son, and the Holy Spirit, 20. and teaching them to obey everything I have commanded you. And surely I am with you to the very end of the age."

The Ripple Effect of the Great Commission

Growing up, I lived by a creek that went through my town. Its name was Big Creek. I often rode my bike on the trails and found rocks to throw into the water. When I was taking my break, I would try to find the smoothest rock and see how many times I could skip it across the water. Imagine a single stone cast into a tranquil pond – its impact extends far beyond the initial splash, sending ripples that touch every corner of the water's expanse.

Similarly, the Great Commission set forth by Jesus has rippled through the ages, leaving a legacy of transformation in its wake. The initial command to "go and make disciples" has birthed movements, shaped cultures, and led countless souls to encounter the profound truths of the Gospel. When Jesus made this declaration, it was not just for the disciples but also for those of us who are believers now. Every bounce of the stone is a new area in the great commissions, making ripples to the environment around the world. **Let us not forsake this call as something that once was but instead view it as the legacy we are called to keep going.** Example: Luke 9:23.Then he said to them all: "Whoever wants to be my disciple must deny themselves and take up their cross daily and follow me."

The early church saw this and rallied behind this call. In the Bible, the book of Acts shows two of Jesus' disciples, Peter and John, went to Jerusalem to proclaim the good news of Jesus' resurrection and his promise of eternal life. This is the first evidence of people being sent out after the resurrection and ascension of Jesus Christ, where he proclaimed the great commission.

We see through the Scripture the widespread Evangelism of the early converts of Jesus became the early Church. The early Church was responsible for the funding and the widespread adoption of the Gospel of Jesus Christ. This was not just church leaders but converts who shared the good news with their friends, family, and neighbors. We can look in Scripture for the example set by Paul, Peter, and many others who have traveled to their parts of the world to be a witness to others in the ancient world. Because of everyday Christians doing this work, we see how the Gospel spreads so widely. Many home churches were created through the early Church. These churches were regular Christians opening their homes to others to share the Gospel.

Skipping to the 1700s, with the age of Enlightenment, many new forms of Evangelism were developed, such as mass printing and tracts. This period saw a significant rise in Evangelism, emphasizing widespread outreach to urban and rural areas. Churches began to use mass distribution of tracts and pamphlets to spread the Gospel. In the late 1800s and early 1900s, revivals were quite popular in the United States. These revivals emphasized sharing the gospel message. Many of those who attended would be "converted" and go out and share their newfound faith. The 19th century saw tremendous growth in evangelical revivalism and the use of Evangelism by religious movements. As the century progressed, migration, changing economic and industrial patterns, and the spread of literacy enabled revivalism and other evangelical efforts to reach far and wide across North America.

During the Second Great Awakening (1800 – 1830), a period of religious revivals throughout the United States, saw the emergence of the camp meeting. A large assembly of people to worship and participate in church activities over several days and nights. Camp Meetings were a popular form of Evangelism, and attendance often included entire families. Smaller but equally effective outdoor revivals also occurred in more densely populated locations, reaching large numbers of people in a particular area through preaching, music, and other activities. With the exception of the mid-century lull in religious revivals, the pattern of outdoor revivals, blessings, and tent revivals continued through the later decades of the 19th century.

Billy Graham and Oral Roberts: Two Pillars in the Evolution of Evangelism in the modern area.

Evangelism, the practice of spreading the Christian faith, has seen a fascinating evolution over the centuries, shaped by charismatic individuals who have left an indelible mark on the history of Christianity. Among these figures, two towering giants stand out: Billy Graham and Oral Roberts. These men, with their unique styles and approaches, played pivotal roles in shaping modern Evangelism as we know it today.

Billy Graham: Evangelist to the Masses

Often referred to as "America's Pastor" Graham's ministry gained national attention in 1949 during a series of revival meetings in Los Angeles. It was here he honed his signature preaching style, which combined powerful, heartfelt messages with an unwavering commitment to Scripture. The "Canvas Cathedral" revival meetings in Los Angeles, where Graham preached under a massive tent, drew large crowds, and captured the imaginations of many. It marked the beginning of his journey to become one of the most recognizable evangelists worldwide. One of the key aspects of Billy Graham's ministry was his focus on inclusivity. He was a unifying figure in the realm of Evangelism, working diligently between denominational lines. His "Christ for all" approach meant he did not dwell on theological intricacies but instead presented a simple message of faith and salvation, making it accessible to people from all walks of life.

Billy Graham was a pioneer in the use of mass media. His radio and television broadcasts reached millions of homes, further expanding his outreach. Graham's embrace of technology and media brought Christ's message into people's homes worldwide. They set a precedent for future evangelists to leverage contemporary communication tools. Graham's legacy also includes a commitment to social issues and civil rights. He was known for his stand against racial segregation and his refusal to preach to segregated audiences. He had a unique ability to bridge divides and used his influence to promote unity making him a forerunner in the movement for racial justice within the Christian community.

In essence, Billy Graham's ministry revolutionized Evangelism in several ways: through his mass appeal, his inclusive approach, and his innovative use of media. His ability to reach people across the globe and between denominational boundaries significantly influenced the evolution of Evangelism into a more modern, interconnected, and accessible practice.

Oral Roberts: The Healing Evangelist

Oral Roberts, another prominent figure in the world of Evangelism, is renowned for his unique approach to ministry, focusing on faith healing and divine miracles. Born on January 24, 1918, in Pontotoc County, Oklahoma, Roberts experienced a profound spiritual encounter as a young man, which he believed was a divine call to preach the Gospel and heal the sick. Roberts' ministry was characterized by an emphasis on the miraculous. He claimed God spoke to him and told him to "Take my healing power to your generation." This led to the establishment of the Oral Roberts Evangelistic Association in 1947. Through his extensive healing campaigns, televised broadcasts, and crusades Roberts gained national and international recognition.

One of the central aspects of Oral Roberts' ministry was his belief in the power of faith healing. He encouraged his followers to have faith that God could heal them of physical and emotional ailments. Roberts' faith healing meetings attracted massive crowds, often filling stadiums to capacity, and drew the attention of skeptics and believers alike. His integration of television into his ministry was a pioneering move. His program, "Oral Roberts Presents," was one of the first religious programs to be aired on a major network. This provided him with a platform to reach millions of people with his message of healing and salvation. The use of mass media brought the message of faith healing to an even broader audience, and it helped shape the landscape of televangelism, a prominent feature of modern Evangelism.

Oral Roberts' ministry had a lasting impact on the way people perceived and practiced healing in Christianity.

While his faith healing approach was met with both enthusiasm and skepticism, it played a significant role in the evolution of charismatic and Pentecostal Christianity, as well as the broader Christian healing movement. The legacy of Oral Roberts extends to the realm of Christian education. He founded Oral Roberts University in 1963, which aimed to provide a Christian education emphasizing faith and learning integration. This institution remains a testament to his vision of equipping future leaders in the Christian community. This is my favorite college and my alma mater.

The ministries of Billy Graham and Oral Roberts played pivotal roles in the evolution of Evangelism as we know it today. Billy Graham's mass appeal, inclusive approach, and use of media revolutionized the practice of Evangelism by making it more accessible and interdenominational. Oral Roberts, on the other hand, introduced a strong emphasis on faith healing, miracles, and divine interventions, which significantly impacted charismatic and Pentecostal Christianity, as well as the broader Christian healing movement. Their legacies continue to shape the landscape of Evangelism in the 21st century, with their influence still evident in the way modern evangelists approach their calling – bridging the spiritual and the technological, the miraculous and the mundane, to spread the message of Christianity to a diverse and interconnected world.

Today, Evangelism remains essential to spreading the Gospel of Jesus Christ. Modern forms of Evangelism, including the Internet, social media, and other digital formats, are paving the way for new and innovative ways of spreading the Gospel. Although revivals may seem old-fashioned, outdoor revivals remain an effective evangelistic tool for sharing the Gospel. Thousands of outdoor revivals are still held today. Although the styles and approaches to Evangelism may change, technology continues to revolutionize how revivals are conducted. Evangelism will always be an essential part of spreading the Gospel.

It is widely known that the word 'evangelism' refers to sharing one's faith with another person. Oxford's online definition states, "It is spreading the Christian Gospel through public preaching or personal witness. Evangelism is the idea of spreading the news about a religion or a company brand. It is most commonly associated with Christianity and refers to extending the story and message of the life of Jesus Christ to impact people's beliefs and lead them to adopt a Christian worldview, accepting Jesus as Lord and Savior," (who died on the cross for sins and rose again). The reason why Evangelism is so closely identified with Christianity is that, within the Christian religion, it is thought as a mandate and core principle of the faith. Evangelism is at the church's and Christianity's core because of Jesus' commands to his disciples, This is something that we, as the Church, are called to live out and dare I say daily.

Let's take this a step further and talk about the word "gospel." It is a central concept in Christianity, and it derives its origins from the Greek word "evangelion" (εὐαγγέλιον). To understand the importance of the word, it's essential to explore its Greek roots and how it has been integral to the Christian faith. The Greek word "evangelion" is a compound word, comprised of two key elements: "eu" (εὖ) and "angelion" (ἀγγέλιον). The prefix "eu" means "good" or "well," and "angelion" signifies a message or news. When combined, "evangelion" means "good news" or "glad tidings." This fundamental word evangelism captures the essence of the Christian message, as the Gospel is indeed a proclamation of the good news of Jesus Christ, His teachings, His life, His sacrifice, and the hope of salvation through faith in Him.

In the New Testament of the Christian Bible, the term "evangelion" is used extensively, and it is frequently associated with the writings of the four evangelists: Matthew, Mark, Luke, and John, who authored the Gospels of the Bible. These books, bearing their names, serve as foundational texts for Christianity, and recount the life, teachings, and significance of Jesus Christ. They are, in essence, the written records of the "good news" of Christ's ministry, crucifixion, and resurrection.

The Christian adoption of "evangelion" reflects a theological and spiritual transformation, where the message of Jesus Christ is considered the ultimate and eternal good news. Through Jesus' life, teachings, death, and resurrection, humanity finds salvation and reconciliation with God, making this "good news" distinct from any other announcement in human history. The Gospel is not just about a proclamation; it is a transformative message that offers redemption, hope, and the promise of eternal life.

As the Christian faith spread throughout the ancient world and beyond, the term "evangelion" became synonymous with the teachings and message of Jesus, giving rise to the idea of the four canonical Gospels in the New Testament. These writings serve as the cornerstone of Christian belief, encapsulating the essence of the Christian faith. Thus, the connection between "gospel" and "evangelion" underscores the central role of good news in Christianity and reflects the profound impact of Greek linguistic roots on the development of Christian theology.

While the roots of the word "gospel" in the Greek "evangelion" reveal the transformative message of Christ central to the Christian faith, the practice of Evangelism takes on various forms and roles. Many people tend to associate the responsibility of spreading the Gospel solely with pastors or priests, sometimes exempting the congregation from active involvement. While it is true that ministers and evangelists play a vital role in equipping the Church, as Ephesians 4:11-12 emphasizes, this perspective doesn't fully align with the core principles of Christianity. Western culture tends to view the sharing of the Gospel as the exclusive duty of those in ministry, influenced by a corporate mentality that has spread into the Church. The analogy of the Church as a business and its leaders as responsible for growth has somewhat distorted the early Christian concept of believers sharing the message of Jesus. However, it is crucial to remember that those who attend Church are not merely attendees; we are the embodiment of the Church itself. Thus, the focus should shift from corporate structures and government regulations to the early Church's mindset, where every follower of Jesus was a participant in sharing the Gospel.

The explosive growth of the early Church after Christ's resurrection was not due solely to the preaching of the twelve apostles. Instead, it resulted from everyday people, the Church who came to know the Lord and those who shared their newfound faith with their households and others in their influence. NIV Acts 2:46-47 **46**, "Every day they continued to meet together in the temple courts. They broke bread in their homes and ate together with glad and sincere hearts,**47** praising God and enjoying the favor of all the people. And the Lord added to their number daily those who were being saved."

This led to the growth of the Church. This is also "marketplace ministry," which occurs when people share their faith while they experience life with others. This can include activities like shopping, working, inviting others over for a meal and sharing life experiences. In ancient cultures, hospitality was a significant aspect of life, as it was a way to show honor, service, and sacrifice to others. By inviting others into relational intimacy, the ministry could happen naturally and from a place of honor, service, and sacrifice. Today, Christians can still live this way, taking Christ to the workplace and being living examples of His truth. Sharing the Gospel with others and showing hospitality. By finding ways to bring honor and sacrifice to others, Christians can live out the Gospel and be an example to those around them. Evangelism will look different and be performed differently by everyone; some people are going to preach from a stage. The most effective type of Evangelism often happens in the lives of people we share life with. A biblical example of effective personal Evangelism is the story of the woman at the well, which can be found in John 4:5-30.

Jesus and his disciples came upon the well outside of the town of Sychar in Samaria during mid-day. The disciples entered the city to get food, leaving Jesus "resting" at the well. A woman came to the well which was unusual as it was understood that women would gather water in the morning when the weather was cooler. Jesus started a conversation with her, which took her off guard because he was a Jew and she was a Samaritan. Jews and Samaritans did not get along, with Samaritans being viewed as unclean and of lesser value of bloodline.

Jesus went straight to the heart of these cultural, racial, and gender issues by asking the woman for water. He then spoke to her about the gift of living water, which would be a well of eternal life inside of her. The woman asked Jesus to give her this living water so she would not have to come to the well daily. Jesus told her to go get her husband when she asked for the water. The woman told Jesus she had no husband, and he told her she had had five husbands and was not currently married to the man she was with. This moment of truth and love showed the woman her sin and her need for living water, which was Jesus himself. The woman recognized Jesus as a prophet and brought up the cultural issue of where they should worship. Jesus explained true worshipers would worship the Father in spirit and in truth. The woman said she believed in a coming messiah and that when he came, he would explain all things. Jesus told her, "I am He." The woman left her water bucket and ran back into town, telling everyone she thought she had met the Messiah.

This story exemplifies how being a personal witness can happen in the lives of people who share lives. Immediately after encountering Christ, she went to tell everyone that this man knew all her sins and told her everything she had done wrong. She shared this with the townspeople, who looked down on her, but gathered to go meet Jesus at the well. This woman was one of the first evangelists in the Bible, and her "style" of Evangelism was invitational. She shared her experiences with Jesus and of sin and how this man knew everything and offered her living water – directing people to him. She had no training, and her boldness came from an encounter with Jesus. She shared the news of the Messiah with those who looked down on her and shamed her. She used her life, sin, and encounter with Jesus to share his love with those she lived with by inviting others to Him. This is a fantastic moment in her life because she was not at the well in the morning with the other women. She was there during the heat of the day because she felt shame as an outcast for her sin, and did not want to be around the other women. Yet, after encountering Jesus, she used her life and story to draw others to Jesus.

We all have a bit of the woman at the well in us, as we have all sinned and done wrong. By experiencing Jesus' love and forgiveness, we can share our struggles, and how Jesus has met us where we are with others. This style of Evangelism is most impactful when done through living life with others and is something we, as the Church, are called to do. You don't have to be perfect to talk to others about Christ. That's not what makes a person a hypocrite.

Another effective style of Evangelism is meeting strangers, encouraging them, and witnessing to them. This style is best for those who are natural encouragers and whose love language is words of affirmation. It's also suitable for those who receive words of knowledge from the Lord, such as sensing God is telling them something about a person. This is similar to Jesus' style in the story of the woman at the well, where he knew about her husband's situation, and he revealed himself to her through these words of knowledge.

Even if you don't have a direct word from the Lord, you can still operate in love and encourage people in the way you discern is best, or use scriptures that are inspiring to lead into a conversation about God's love for them and why God sent Jesus to die for their sins. This is another effective way to break the ice and provide encouragement in a world that can be so discouraging.

CHAPTER 2

Styles of Evangelism

It is important to remember that Evangelism is not just for
pastors and teachers in the faith. We are all the church;
each has unique gifts and abilities and can reach people
others can't. God has uniquely positioned you to be where
you are for the restoration of other people's spirits in Christ.
You are far more critical in Christ's body and Evangelism
ministry than you realize.

There are many styles of Evangelism: Here are just a
few. **Testimony, relational, invitational, service, intellectual, street evangelism, and digital Evangelism.** While
each of us may have a bent toward one or more of these
styles, it is still important to grow in the area where God
has given us the ability to share the gospel. Some of these
styles can overlap when you do ministry, for example, relational and invitational Evangelism or testimony and street
evangelism. Mixing and matching styles can strengthen
your purpose and the effects of Evangelism. Here are some

different styles of Evangelism you may consider adding into your own life.

Storytelling/ Testimony

A lot of believers have a testimony. It's a story about how Jesus impacted their life and changed them. They often describe how Jesus helped them through difficult times and what they learned during this season of their life. A good storyteller is charismatic, vulnerable, and authentic. Through telling their story, they connect with others and help the listener relate to their experiences. Compelling storytellers know how to use dramatic pauses and timing to captivate their audience while staying true to the story. They use words to paint vivid pictures in the minds of their listeners; they understand their audience and how to craft their comments to make the story relatable and memorable. This empowers the listener to face their own challenges in life.

Without rewriting my testimony, I want to reference the story of losing my daughter and why Evangelism is so important to me. That testimony is an example of taking a real story. Through the process of the pain and grief, God redeemed it into something I can share with others, and it brings them life, hope, and, in some cases, joy. While your testimony does not have to be like mine, I encourage you to look at your life and see where God has shown up. These are the moments you can share as testimonies. I have many different stories/testimonies in my life based on a wide variety of topics. I suggest you start with one story and one topic. Craft the story truthfully, get good at sharing it, add another testimony and keep growing your testimonies inventory. Think of experiences you have had several times and how God has shown himself to you through these experiences. Over time, you can create an index of personal testimonies which will reach people in different situations. Stories you can pull from to ministry to their needs.

Here's a helpful exercise to find testimonies you may not be aware of: If you prefer physical notes, get a large white poster board and four different colors of sticky notes (green, blue, and red). If you prefer digital, go to https:// trello.com. The blue sticky notes represent chapters in your life, like the headings of specific seasons – for example, four years of college. The yellow sticky notes represent events, stories, or memories (good or bad), losses, people, circumstances, etc. Red represents a negative event in your life, and green represents a life lesson you may have learned from a negative or even a positive one in yellow. Start as far back in your life as you can remember and take notes about people and events that have happened, and things you learned then or things you learned reflecting on the occasion. When I did this, not only did this bring healing to my own life, but it helped me start mapping out my life from about three years old to my 35-year-old self. I have done this exercise about three times in the past 15 years, once every five years.

I learned this practice through a coaching program called "Your One Degree." This will take you hours or even days, but it's important to do. You are stewarding your story by going through this process. I did my first two on large paper and the last one digitally. I found the digital version to be faster; I could add different colors to one block to identify what that block means in my life. After engaging in this process, I reflected on my life and noticed patterns had emerged in different areas. I found similar stories have been repeated that cause pain. I now realize I knew some of my testimonies and what I could speak about. I identified key lessons in my life that I could craft my story around. I encourage you to do this exercise. Sharing testimonies is a fantastic way to connect with people and draw them in to experience the power of God through your own life by relating it to them.

With that being said, like anything good, satan will try to twist and make evil out of it. Some traps that can hurt a person with the gift of storytelling include exaggerating the story to make it more impactful. When people see this, they feel this person is not being truthful. Or this person's story could be more consistent from one conversation to the next. It is easy to make a story about yourself and get gratification and importance from it. That thinking can lead to embellishing a story. Don't do that. Make the story about God's goodness and what God taught you through the experience. To take testimonies/stories one step further, you can show how they relate to the other person and what they can glean from it. Paul's inspiration when writing the Philippians' church is an excellent example. While he was in chains and could have written the letter about himself and his suffering, he instead promoted God and how God was using the circumstances. He gave glory to God, and it encouraged that body of believers who were bolder about sharing their faith.

People with the gift of storytelling may often seem misunderstood and questioned about their life choices. If the story is not crafted well, this person can appear self-centered and self-absorbed. This person may also tend only to tell stories about themselves when talking to others and try to impress people with different events in their life. You know the feeling, trying to one-up others with your story. However, let's not throw the baby out with the bathwater.

To the person who is a gifted storyteller, don't let the traps of your personality hinder the incredible gift God has given you. Just be self-aware when you start operating from the pitfalls of your gifting versus the actual gift. I am speaking from experience. Your story is good enough to share if you have sought God on how to share it. You don't have to make things up to make the story more impactful. This gifting of Evangelism can happen in many settings. It is great for one-on-one conversations or in a group setting. Story or testimony evangelism is excellent for digital Evangelism or even building relationships with others because there is a sense of vulnerability to it. Sharing it in front of a group of people can also be encouraging and set the tone for a sermon.

Relational Evangelism:

This style of ministry is most impactful by being present in your daily life with purpose and recognizing God has called you to minister to those around you, including at work, daycare, and restaurants where you are a regular. It involves connecting with neighbors meaningfully and being present at dinners, family reunions, or parent-teacher meetings. Relational Evangelism is always possible when you are open to connecting with others around you. We must all show up in the lives of those around us and not just be an example but also bring the message of Jesus Christ into our everyday lives. Remember **people are not an inconvenience** in your day or plans but are sometimes put there by God for you to interact with them. **We often rush past the very people Jesus wants us to recognize. Be a blessing wherever you go, even if it costs you something.**

Here are some tips to help you further develop this relational Evangelism: Focus on making a few new relationships which naturally fit into your life. For example, if you go to the same grocery store, you'll see the same employees consistently. Target a few people you can build a relationship with over time. After a few months of consistent visits you can develop deeper relationships with these individuals. Relationships that transcend to coffee, lunch, an exchange of numbers, or at a minimum, being able to have a little conversation with them at their work. This works because it is a natural progression and part of your routine at the store rather than something you must manufacture actively. I believe God will show you who those people are. If, for some reason, you don't feel like God is leading you, then find some yourself; there is no harm in that.

For example, I have been going to the same Thai restaurant since 2008, owned by two partners, one who says he is a Christian and the other who says he is a non-Christian. I have built a relationship with the owners since 2008, when they opened, which is conveniently located by Oral

Roberts University, where I attended college. I would often witness to the non-Christian owner. I am unaware if he ever accepted Jesus as lord and savior. He went on to sell his position in the business to his partner. However, there have been many years of friendship ministry and seed planting in his life. I had a hairstylist who was also a non-Christian. I don't preach to these people when I visit them. I show up, be friendly, build relationships, and ask them reflective questions about life – and I talk about Jesus. Not all the time, but sometimes. When I do, I casually get into the – gospel message, why it's important to me, and why I believe it. I always try to be led by God in these moments.

One of the other things I learned through Evangelism when I first started was to pray for open doors of opportunity to witness to people. Suppose you pray that prayer; be ready to act on it. God will help you see opportunities that are commonly missed. These relational and evangelistic opportunities are everywhere. When you pray this prayer, expect to see opportunities. This is why it is essential to slow down in life so you can see them. Because if you are rushing through life, **you will miss the people and the opportunity because you are looking past them, not for them.** These opportunities don't often present themselves in some big, holy, religious moment; they are usually small and easily overlooked in the rush of everyday life. You can avoid seeing people as an inconvenience by adding extra time to your schedule for relational Evangelism to happen. This will help you focus on connecting with others in a meaningful way rather than just getting the task you set out to do. **People are God's creation whom he loves and**

places his image on. When looking at others, you are looking at the face of God.

Have a hit list. A hit list consists of people who are closer to you in a relationship and who don't know the Lord or need to grow deeper with Him. Create a list of these individuals in your life. This can help you take more deliberate action with those closer to you. Targeting these people takes intentionality and devotion, but it is worthwhile. Pray for each person on your list, asking God to soften their heart, lift any deception, and bring them to a deeper understanding of the truth according to His Word. Pray that God would work on their hearts and bring situations into their lives that lead them to an openness to the Lord. Relational Evangelism often involves sacrifice, as building relationships with others may require us to make sacrifices to help them. This overlap of relational and sacrificial is a valuable aspect of this style of ministry.

I remember back in high school, there was a new student named Omar who came from out of state. His reputation was that he was a Hispanic gangster who may have killed a person or two. These were just unfounded rumors but believed. Most students were scared of him. He had a look of anger on his face that made most people afraid to talk to him. He was already a father in high school as well. I wanted to witness him, and as I prayed for a way to do that, I heard God say, "Go give him a bro hug." A bro hug is not a regular hug. It starts with a handshake, grabs each other's hand, and pulls the other close with a pair of arms between the two, avoiding getting too close. One arm pats the other person's back no more than three times. The first time I went to Omar and hugged him, it caught him off guard. I thought I would share the gospel with him next time, but when I saw him later, I heard God say to give him another bro hug.

As time went on, every time I saw Omar in the hall, we would give each other a bro hug. This went on for the rest of my senior year in high school. Fast forward, as I was getting ready to leave for college, I felt downcast about not knowing if I made a difference in the lives of others at my high school. I was often bullied and thought my hardships were for nothing. One night in August, the day before I was to move to Tulsa, Oklahoma, I was in the McDonald's parking lot having a pity party When an older man walked up to me, convinced he was Jesus Christ, and tried to get me to follow him. Omar, driving by, saw this, pulled in, and started talking to me about how this guy was fake and how I should not believe him, which I did not. Omar did not know I was a Christian for most of our time in high school together. He started asking himself questions about me after many hugs. Why is this guy different? Why is he so happy when so many people are passive and afraid of him? Eventually, he connected with local community pastors who knew me and my heart for the Lord.

Through conversation, I came up, and they told him about my faith in Jesus, which made me different. Omar went on to accept Jesus as his Lord and Savior, bringing his parents, girlfriend, and child to church with him, and over time, his whole family came to know the Lord. Showing up consistently with a hug started softening his heart and led him to accept the Lord. Remember, in Evangelism, there are three areas: planting seed, watering that seed, and harvesting that seed. Discern which one God is calling you to do for each person in your life; their life, story, and process of coming to know the Lord are all different.

Relational Evangelism can be challenging for some individuals who may not be naturally outgoing. This is okay, as anyone can work on this skill by simply being present in the lives of those around them. If you excel in this area of relationships, you may possess certain traits. People who are successful in relational Evangelism tend to be outgoing and enjoy being around others or even meeting new people. They is no such thing as a stranger and possess strong communication skills, making others feel at ease when speaking with them. In my case, I can also make people feel uncomfortable. They are adept at starting conversations, connecting with others, and seeing their needs. One skill set of this type of person is the ability to manage a variety of friendships and relationships. They often initiate relationships and should not feel bad about it, as others may not have this gift.

Additionally, they may enjoy participating in community events. This person can also quickly feel alone because they don't feel like people are reaching out to them. I have learned this lesson many times over the years. I have the skills to manage a lot of relationships, and I am the one often doing all the reaching out. I have learned this is a skill and that only some have it. So don't let your skill in this area become a tool that Satan uses as a lie to make you feel alone because other people are not reaching out to you. He will do anything to prevent you from using your gift. For example, "John Jacob Jingle Heimer Schmidt" never calls me, so I will stop calling him. This is what Satan wants.

Another downside of this trait and gift is that they may open up to people too quickly, which can be a turn-off for others. Or feel too comfortable sharing things about their life that should be confidential. Due to their ability to meet many new people quickly and form relationships, it is essential to learn how to form deeper connections with others over time. This person and skill set may trust others too quickly, which can be a painful experience. God also opens doors for deep relationships rapidly. Learn to discern the difference between the two by practicing the skill set of building relationships with many different people.

It is important to understand that people are open to discussing Christianity in the right environment. For this person, it tends to be on an individual basis. I found some statistics From the Barna research group on their website. https://www.barna.com/research/opportunities-for-faith-sharing/

"For instance, non-Christians and lapsed Christians who say spirituality plays a significant role in their life, and/or that they have unanswered spiritual questions (more "spiritually curious" types), tend to be more open to a variety of settings to explore questions of faith. On the other hand, those who say otherwise (less "spiritually curious" types) are less open. Looking at the data, among all non-Christians and lapsed Christians, three in 10 (30%) say they prefer a "casual, one-on-one conversation." But the percentage is higher among those for whom spirituality is significant (40%) than among those for whom it is not (27%). Similarly, non-Christians and lapsed Christians who agree strongly that they have unanswered spiritual questions are more likely to say they prefer one-on-one conversation (45%) than those who don't have such questions (20%). Overall, settings that prioritize relational interactions tend to be more attractive than approaches that don't, even among those who are inclined toward spirituality."

Invitational Evangelism:

Invitational evangelism is a great starting point if you are new to the faith and need help knowing where to begin. This was exemplified in the woman's story at the well; people did not want anything to do with her. She had poor relationship status with people in her town but invited everyone to meet the man at the well who told her all her sins. Invitational evangelism can be used with other styles of evangelism and involves inviting others to participate in church-related or gospel-related activities, such as attending church services, bible studies, retreats, small groups, or Christian movies. This is the lowest barrier of entry for sharing the gospel with others and is a highly recommended starting point for those unsure of where to begin.

Jesus' ministry began with the invitation, as He called His disciples to Him and invited them to learn and grow under His teachings. They left what they were doing to follow Him, quickly becoming relational evangelism and discipleship. Invitational evangelism can be done with both strangers and people in your life. As a church or ministry, we often create events to attract people and use marketing and invitational evangelism to invite them. Invitational evangelism is a low-barrier entry for sharing the gospel and can be directed toward strangers and people we know.

An example of this type of ministry is when I organized an event as a real estate agent and raised money, and rented out a movie theater to show a preview of a film I can only imagine. This was meant for past clients and referral partners. I also included giveaways such as meal gift cards and a 55-inch TV. At the end of the movie, I shared my testimony. Not many of my intended audience accepted the free movie. Although the event was meant to be private, the event was open to the public on event bright, and the event showed up on the first page of Google when searching for information about the movie in the area. I oversold the theater by 30 tickets and ended up with 15 open seats out of 80.

The event taught me that sometimes, even when no one shows up, God can bring the people He wants to the event. This is illustrated in the Parable of the Wedding Banquet, where the servants were sent to invite those who had been previously invited, but they refused. The host then sent the servants to gather anyone they could find, high or lowly of stature, and the wedding hall was filled with guests. The parable shows that even though many are invited, only a few choose to come. Matthew 22:1-14 and Luke 14:15-24. Creating events to invite people to attend is a good practice for a church, ministry, or individual. Marketing and invitational evangelism are used to attract attendees. These events should aim to share a testimony, make a salvation call, and go deeper in ministry.

I share this wedding banquet and movie theater story because I want you to have realistic expectations regarding invitational evangelism. In the world of ministry, the reason for this type of outreach is noble. However, the majority of people will still be disinterested. Does this mean we don't do this type of ministry? No, we still do it, but with an understanding that the outcome may look different than what we originally envisioned. This does not mean it's a failure.

Another excellent example is what life church did with the Bible app before there were any apps. Life church tried to create software like Facebook for people to do bible studies online, to read the bible, and have a social network aspect to it. They spent much time and money on the program, which failed, but should have done better. Around the time of what seemed to be a failure, the Apple company was coming out with the app store for the iPhone. They had an intern figure out how to make an app and convert the material they created for the other program into what is now the bible app. It was one of the first apps ever created and is, to this day, still one of the most downloaded apps. We never know how God will use our efforts, even if, at first, they seem like a failure to us.

It is hard in America for churches to compete for entertainment value and attraction in a culture with so many entertainment options. I believe this is why we see so many churches struggle to compete in that space. This is why it is essential to not focus on entertaining people but rather be a place where people are encouraged, healed, and find it easier to connect to God and grow in relationship with him. Outreaches through events are different than just trying to attract through entertainment.

Even in the worst of times, God can still use it for his good. Many churches closed their doors and never opened them during covid. I believe COVID-19, while a curse created by men and sin, was also an opportunity for the church. It made many people go digital, which is the lowest barrier of entry for people to attend church online. When making invitations to church, I suggest you invite them to participate in person, but if they can't come in person, encourage them to join online. You could also provide a card with a QR code on the back to make it easy for them to find the church online.

According to Barna Research Group, "the reception a Christian can expect on the other side of an invitation to church may vary. "It might be pretty chilly: Overall, about half of all unchurched adults (52%) – including three-quarters of non-Christians (73%) – wouldn't be interested in any invitation to any church or faith environment. For non-Christians, an online church service viewed alone, is the only activity for which (the percentage is 12%) they would consider participation in. This suggests that formal communal participation, unlike solo spiritual exploration or relational discussion." https://www.barna.com/research/digital-service-invitation/n. This is a starting point for many outside the church.

The Power of Inviting Someone to Church.

As of writing this just yesterday, my wife and I were invited to a friend's church for a Wednesday night service. Although we already attend church, we don't have services on Wednesday nights. Our entire family attended our friend's church. My wife and I with the craziness of having four young children, have been struggling in our marriage. While our current church is great, we realized we need more church in our lives. The new church, being a bigger one, had multiple services throughout the week. We went from attending one service a week to a Sunday service, a Wednesday night service, a Bible study Sunday morning, and sometimes the Saturday church service. Even though Saturday and Sunday services have the same message, I don't know if we did it to get away from our kids or because we needed it. LOL!

Our spirits, by default, were being fed more. A marriage counselor we started seeing to help us communicate better went to that church. Our family engages in more relationships because of the opportunities to be around others more often. It's been about four months since attending our new church at this point of the writing. It has recently become our new church family. People are at different churches for different seasons of one's life. Being invited to attend a Wednesday night service has changed my life and my family. While we have yet to find perfection in our lives, or as close to it as one can achieve, we are doing better in our marriage and family. There is a strong case for being where God wants you to be. Being in a healthy church where your family can grow and heal is extremely important for us as

Christians – and those we invite into the four walls. We, as believers, are also the church and are called to be that for others. We do this by inviting people into our lives to the degree God leads us. With the resources God has given us in our giftings, we minister.

The power of inviting someone to church can be life-changing, whether they are saved or not. A community is a place to help individuals heal, grow, and find their purpose. Not every church is like this, but good ones are out there. And it's important to remember that no church is perfect. So, invite someone to church this week and see its impact on their life. As I edit my book, we have been going to our new church for a year. The difference in our lives has been drastic and has helped us to be better equipped for the challenges we face in life. The new church has given us relationships we have been able to grow in and with – to no longer feel alone, and to be encouraged. This is bearing each other's burdens. All of this came about because of a simple invitation. We were not looking to switch churches. We did not want to change churches. We were going to a great church. God moved us to a different place for a different season of our lives. So don't be afraid to ask people who seem stuck in their ways to go to church or to an event with you. God is working behind the details, and if you feel led by the Lord to make an invitation, do it.

(Author life update) This new church that I described has been a wonderful experience. I have seen my marriage heal and our family grow in ways I don't know would have happened without them. I signed up to get licensed through the Assemblies of God by attending this church. I received my license on February 5th of, 2024. While attending the church, I was looking to get on staff, but there was no availability. I was encouraged to look elsewhere. So I did. I now lead a small church in Jenks, Oklahoma, called River Oaks Christian Church. It's funny to think what a simple invitation to someone's church led to in my family. It was healing, growth, being credentialed, and taking on a pastoral role. Thank you, Mark Rentz, for that invitation.

Service approach

The approach of meeting people's needs and showing up to help them in their time of need can be a powerful form of evangelism. This is often referred to as the "service approach." This approach requires more sacrifice and dedication from the person doing the ministry. Still, it can often open doors in people's lives and build trust. People are often more receptive to hearing about Jesus and his love when they are being served by demonstrating love and care, even at personal cost. This is why the Mormon church is so big on sending out missionaries. They want them to serve the local community and allow elders to talk about Mormonism.

An example of this approach can be seen in the early church after Pentecost, as described in NIV Acts 2. **44:** "All the believers were together and had everything in common. **45** They sold property and possessions to give to anyone who had need." This passage is often taken out of context and used to promote socialism. The argument that everyone shared everything and no one had any possessions of their own is misguided. The truth of this passage is that it is not an example of socialism. The believer, out of their love for others, gave to help others. This was voluntary, not government or church mandated. Socialism is where the government takes away people's property and belongings in this system for "equality purposes." Often, when the government takes in the name of redistributing wealth, it is not given to those in need. It is given to other government programs. What does get distributed is often a tiny fraction of what was acutely taken in the first place.

The sense of community and sacrifice within the church of Acts led to rapid growth as more and more people were drawn to the love and care demonstrated by the believers. It is important to remember that while this approach can be practical, it may require more time, effort, and sacrifice. However, when done with a heart focused on loving and serving others, it can be a powerful tool for sharing the message of Jesus.

In contrast, we see an example of the Kingdom of God in this passage, where believers chose to sell their properties and were willing to give to other believers until all needs were met. This is the example that Jesus set for us on the cross when He gave up His position at the Father's right hand and became a sacrifice for all sin. Jesus took upon himself three major demotions to serve others and God. He is the example that we, as the church, should follow when it comes to serving others. NIV Philippians 2:5-8 5 In your relationships with one another have the same mindset as Christ Jesus: 6 Who, being in very nature God, did not consider equality with God something to be used to his own advantage; 7 rather, he made himself nothing by taking the very nature of a servant, being made in human likeness. 8 And being found in appearance as a man, he humbled himself by becoming obedient to death – even death on a cross!

First, Jesus left heaven; second, he became a bondservant to us all; and third, he died for us. These three areas of his life of serving others resulted in demotion and personal sacrifice.

He lived a life we could not live and was the sacrifice we could not be to have entrance into heaven. Salvation could never be ours without Jesus' sacrificial service to us. You might be thinking, "How can I participate in acts of service if I don't have money?" It doesn't take money to be a blessing to others. You can volunteer your time at a food bank to help feed people. You can mow an older adult's yard, cook a meal for a family that has experienced a tragedy, or organize a meal train for that family. You could even join an outreach program that a church is doing. Living a service lifestyle requires diligence to continuously see the needs of others and help meet those needs. It is so easy to become self-absorbed with what is going on in our life that we don't take time to see the needs of others around.

Our natural state of mind as sinful people is selfishness, so renewing our minds and seeing others before ourselves takes diligence. This is not easy, but we are to be led by the Holy Spirit and do what he leads us to do by the Father's will. By checking in with the Holy Spirit, we can follow and discern God's will when it comes to meeting the needs of others.

In the summer of 2008, I worked at Fathers House church in Tulsa. I worked in a snow cone stand. That church had bought the snow cone stand so I could have a job and stay in Tulsa that summer of college. I made only $500 a month and worked 10-12 hours a day, six days a week. Rip off? No, not even. I had a desire to stay and serve my local church with an internship. But I would also need a flexible summer Job. I had no job, and they created one for me. Thank you so much, Fred, Cookie, and Jon! During this summer, I gained so much ministry experience from that snow cone stand. I ended up spending a lot of time with God, and this was before smartphones. Most hours were spent working on my internship, I only had a few customers. I spent time in prayer and seeking God. One of my main prayers that summer was to see the physical manifestation of Jesus. I heard he did it for others, so why would he not do it for me? I spent much of my time that summer praying that Jesus would manifest himself in my room and that we would be able to have a conversation. After weeks of taking time to pray, I went to Walmart one day after a few hours of prayer. Still, this time, instead of getting in and out as quickly as possible, I noticed people around me more than I have in times past. I saw those in need. I noticed their clothes were dirty and entirely damaged. I noticed other people's lives as I walked through the store and felt that God was talking to me about the people I passed. I saw the mother in front of me had insufficient money for food and diapers and that the cashier was having a hard day. Nothing major happened at Walmart, but I noticed people and their situations more than I ever had in the past. I got back to my room on my day off, and prayed again for Jesus to manifest himself to me, and very quickly, he did. He told me to read.

Matthew 25 (NIV) reads. **31** "When the Son of Man comes in his glory, and all the angels with him, he will sit on his glorious throne.**32** All the nations will be gathered before him, and he will separate the people one from another as a shepherd separates the sheep from the goats. **33** He will put the sheep on his right and the goats on his left. **34** "Then the King will say to those on his right, 'Come, you who are blessed by my Father; take your inheritance, the kingdom prepared for you since the creation of the world. **35** For I was hungry, and you gave me something to eat, I was thirsty, and you gave me something to drink, I was a stranger, and you invited me in, **36** I needed clothes, and you clothed me, I was sick, and you looked after me, I was in prison, and you came to visit me.' **37** "Then the righteous will answer him, 'Lord, when did we see you hungry and feed you, or thirsty and give you something to drink? **38** When did we see you a stranger and invite you in, or needing clothes and clothe you? **39** When did we see you sick or in prison and go to visit you?' **40** "The King will reply, 'Truly I tell you, whatever you did for one of the least of these brothers and sisters of mine, you did for me.' **41** "Then he will say to those on his left, 'Depart from me, you who are cursed, into the eternal fire prepared for the devil and his angels. **42** For I was hungry, and you gave me nothing to eat, I was thirsty, and you gave me nothing to drink, **43** I was a stranger, and you did not invite me in, I needed clothes, and you did not clothe me, I was sick and in prison, and you did not look after me.' **44** "They also will answer,

'Lord, when did we see you hungry or thirsty or a stranger or needing clothes or sick or in prison, and did not help you?' **45** "He will reply, 'Truly I tell you, whatever you did not do for one of the least of these, you did not do for me.' 46 "Then they will go away to eternal punishment, but the righteous to eternal life."

After reading this, God showed me that I have been seeing Jesus and his face but failed to notice it. When I look into the face of other people I see the face of Jesus. How I treat others is how I treat Jesus. God spoke to me and said. **The quickest way to touch the heart of God is by touching other people's lives**. Disregard the idea of being a doormat. We help people who want and need help. We don't aid in someone's addictions. Regardless of their circumstance, when we look at people as a way to see Jesus, we bring value to who God created them to be and see them in their identity with Christ.

There are two reasons I meet the needs of others. Firstly, the Lord is leading me to do so. Secondly, I see the need and have the ability to help so I think, "If not me, then who?" You never need a "Thus saith the Lord" to do good. When God leads you to do something, do it. In the meantime, if you can meet a need, do it. This develops the diligence aspect of always being willing to live a life serving others, which is one way Christians do evangelism. It's like a muscle; the more we exercise it, the stronger it gets. The more we learn how to meet the needs of others, the more we can do so – and love people the way Jesus desires us to. This is also a spiritual journey because it transforms our hearts and minds to be and think like Christ, transforming us into his image and sharing the gospel's good news. The type of people who are called to serve in the body of Christ is everyone. Not everyone may have a natural gift for acts of service, but we can all still pay attention to this area. Everyone has a role to play in serving others and meeting their needs. It may require more effort for some, while for others, it may come more naturally. Some individuals may benefit from networking groups and learn about making connections with others.

Some people may have a strong sense of empathy toward others' and their situations in life. Some may have specific skills like plumbing, electrical work, handyperson work, lawncare, mentoring, hair styling, cooking, or cleaning. We can use the gifts and talent that God has given us to serve other people; and use that as an opportunity to share the love of God for the redemption of sin through a life surrendered to Jesus. Individuals who naturally have the ministry gift in acts of service may face certain challenges. They may feel pressure to serve and meet the needs of others beyond their capacity, or they may get emotionally attached to others' needs and feel hurt or hopeless when they can't help on a larger scale. They may feel guilty if they can't help someone in need. This person might be easily manipulated by others to feel their need and be taken advantage of. You might want to change the world in an area but only find you need more resources. **You can change the world by changing one person's life because, for that person, their world changes.**

In conclusion, acts of service are a way for Christians to evangelize, and everyone in the body of Christ has a role to play, regardless of their natural gifts. By serving others and meeting their needs, individuals can strengthen their muscles of service and learn to be more diligent in living a life of service to others. The most outstanding example of this is communion. Jesus was telling us to take communion in remembrance of him. Not just as a symbolic gesture of drinking wine and eating crackers – but to live life like the communion by placing ourselves in situations to be broken and poured out for others. This is the truest example of taking communion one can do. I believe this is why we have this scripture from Luke 9:23-24 NIV **23** Then he said to them all: "Whoever wants to be my disciple must deny themselves and take up their cross daily and follow me. **24** For whoever wants to save their life will lose it, but whoever loses their life for me will save it. When the church rises up and meets the needs of others, we will look like the early church and the way God intended us to view each other.

Intellectual Evangelism: Sharing the good news in truth and love.

Can I be honest with you? This is my favorite form of evangelism, but it's also the one I'm least gifted in. I love watching deep thinkers of God's word dialogue with non-believers and destroy their false views with biblical and historical facts. This form of evangelism is often referred to as "apologetics." According to Merriam-Webster, apologetics is "systematic argumentative discourse in defense (as of a doctrine) or a branch of theology devoted to the defense of the divine origin and authority of Christianity."

Some well-known apologetics include C.S. Lewis, Tim Keller, and Josh McDowell.

As Christians, the Bible instructs us to be able to give an account of our beliefs when asked. It's important to have a good understanding of the gospel and the Bible as a whole, as it is the living word of God and should be integrated into our daily lives. This is done over time and by the discipline of studying God's word and cultural relevance in the scriptures. Intellectual evangelism goes beyond just knowing the Bible. It's the ability to defend and explain it, cross-reference it, and make convincing arguments without using the Bible.

Apologetics is a branch of theology concerned with defending religious beliefs by answering questions and addressing objections to these beliefs. The goal is to show that these beliefs are reasonable and supportable. There are different approaches to apologetics, focusing on defending specific beliefs. In contrast, others support religion as a whole. One can use a range of styles within apologetics depending on the situation, goals, and truths they wish to convey. The most common approaches include:

1. Showing Evidence: This involves presenting factual evidence that supports the belief or point being made, such as historical or scientific evidence.
2. Reasoning: This involves using logic and reason to show your beliefs are logical and understandable.
3. Objection Handling: This involves addressing specific objections or questions people have about

your views and attempt to discredit why they are not valid.

4. Testimony: involves sharing personal experiences, and how they relate to your beliefs.

When engaging in apologetics, it's essential to be respectful and open to dialogue, even if you disagree with someone's beliefs. Avoid being condescending to the other person's ideas, as this approach is ineffective in most situations. It's also essential to be well-informed about the Christian life, biblical principles, and the objections people may have to them, So you can defend them and lovingly present the truth.

This next part is significant to not misunderstand what I am saying. Christians must believe that the Bible is the infallible word of God and it is the absolute authority and instructions given to us by God. We believe the Bible is full of teachings, is a historical document, and is now proving to be scientific also. When witnessing out of a relationship, I would say use the Bible or even openly share the gospel. When it comes to debating, that is another story. I have often tried to use the Bible as the source of authority in which I speak when debating atheists. I had always failed because an atheist does not believe that the Bible is the authority. Therefore, if I use it, I discredit myself to them.

Firstly, the Bible is a religious text based on the followers of Christianity and Judaism who have faith that the scriptures are God's inspired words. The nonbeliever views the Bible as having no evidence of it being authentic. It is not a scientific or historical document and can't be used to prove or disprove a point in a debate. Therefore, using the Bible as a source of authority in a discussion can be ineffective as it may not be accepted by someone who does not share the same faith.

Secondly, using the Bible as a source of authority assumes that the person being debated accepts the validity of the Bible as an authoritative source. However, this is only sometimes the case. People from different religious backgrounds may not accept the Bible as an authoritative source of information. When engaging in debate or intellectual evangelism, I have found it most helpful to study areas like quantum physics and other historical documents to prove the Bible is accurate. And though science is catching up with the Bible, I try to find ways to talk to people without using the Bible as an authority when in a debate setting. A good place to begin this training is through an apologetics class or watching debates on subjects you are interested in. If you are debating ethics I would use the Bible as a credible moral source.

People with the gift of apologetics have a good understanding of other religions', world views. This person knows the major differences between those views and Christianity. They might be a person who is more politically bent and used to talking about differences of opinion. They may be knowledgeable about science and be able to use it to prove God's existence. This type of person is often an intellectual skilled in memorizing concepts, ideas, and facts and can put complex thoughts into an easy conversation. They tend to be well-spoken, good writers, and strong-willed.

However, their lack of empathy and strong sense of truth can sometimes make them appear snobbish and give off a pretentious vibe. They may need help breaking down complex concepts for others who are not as gifted in deep thought to be effective in intellectual evangelism. It is important to approach others as a consistent learner and not as if you are a know-it-all and are talking down to them. This person often thinks they are right and carries this attitude in relationships and conversations. Speaking from experience, if I am empathetic towards the other person and come off as a fellow learner, I have had better success.

All styles of evangelism are vital as they meet the needs and diversity of people's designs. Intellectual evangelism is crucial for those of us who struggle, as many cultures have turned away from God and Christianity to rely on science, government and propaganda. Intellectual evangelists have the potential to be strong critical thinkers and influential people, like Joseph in the Bible, who went from being a slave to a prisoner to second in command of all of Egypt. We have others like Meshack, Shadrack and Abednego as well as Daniel. Intellectual evangelists also need to be strong in character and have high endurance levels to withstand persecution when others may cringe. Intellectual evangelists can influence and shape culture, just like Jesus did when talking to the woman at the well.

Jesus replied in John 4:21-25 NIV "Believe me, dear woman, the time is coming when it will no longer matter whether you worship the Father on this mountain or in Jerusalem. You Samaritans know very little about the one you worship, while the Jews know all about Him, for salvation comes through the Jews. But the time is coming – indeed, it's here now – when true worshipers will worship the Father in spirit and truth. The Father is looking for those who will worship Him that way, for God is Spirit and those who worship Him must worship in spirit and truth."

For this gift of intellectual evangelism is to shape the hearts and minds of others, it will require individuals to worship God in spirit and truth. Be connected to the Lord, and let the Holy Spirit guide you in life and conversation. Know the truth so you can live and speak it. We are all called to live this way. Some may be more gifted than others, but those who are not may need to do extra work. Those who are less talented should understand that this will not diminish their role in the body of Christ, but in due time, they need to be able to give an account of their beliefs.

Street Evangelism:

When people think of street ministry, they envision sign-carrying, megaphone-yelling individuals screaming at people about going to hell if they don't repent for their sins. While there is truth in the message, this depiction is a great disservice to the actual community they are trying to serve. I have encountered such people while doing street ministry. Not only did it hinder my work, I chose to leave because it negatively impacted what Jesus wanted to do. I wanted to avoid being associated with that style of ministry.

Jesus spoke the truth in love to many people. He came from a place of compassion, meeting people in their situations, and spoke truth to them that transformed their hearts and minds. He ministered to people in physical ways, such as healing, and his greatest works came from people's lives being transformed by His presence.

I think of Zacchaeus the tax collector and how Jesus told him He would eat with him at his house, which would have been forbidden. Jews disowned Jews who collected taxes because they often cheated people out of their money for their financial gain and were siding with the Roman government's oppression of the Jewish community. In meeting Jesus Zacchaeus had true repentance and gave back (and more) to people from whom he had stolen. Only through meeting Jesus can this kind of heart transformation happen in someone. His heart changed in the time it took him to get down from the tree. When people encounter the presence of Jesus, their hearts can immediately change. This is why presence-based ministry is so important and is not being work of the flesh.

This is the kind of street ministry I like to do. Where when meeting strangers you show them Jesus and their lives transform – where healing takes place in their hearts and minds. One of my favorite stories of street ministry is when I was going out to eat with my wife. She had a business trip in Oklahoma City, about an hour and a half from where we live. She had to stay overnight so at the last minute I decided I wanted to go with her. We arrived in Oklahoma City, unpacked our bags in the hotel room, and looked for places nearby to eat. As we walked into the restaurant, the hostess asked us where we wanted to be seated; I heard the name "Emily" in my head.

I said, "Sit us in Emily's section," to which she responded, "Do you know Emily?" I said, "No." She asked,

"Did you hear about Emily?" I said, "No." Then she asked, "Why are you requesting her?" I said, "Because God said so." The host said, "Well, I don't think she's working today." I said, "Okay, no worries." We got seated, and guess who took over our section? Emily. She was starting her shift just as we got there. I didn't know, Emily. I had never met her or heard of her, but God knew who she is, and it was Him wanting to connect with her. Emily knew she was requested to be our server but did not know why. I immediately knew something was going on and God wanted me to minister to her, I just didn't know in what capacity. As she served us, I begin learning about her life and her situation.

I told her she has a hurtful relationship with a male in her life, perhaps a boyfriend or Father. She begin to share stories that had shaped her life, including how she emancipated herself at 16, and left home – her Father was struggling with dementia. Throughout the evening, we talked more, and I was able to minister to her heart through words of knowledge. Her response and curiosity to how I knew certain things about her life created a desire in her to know why this moment was happening to her.

I told her I had no idea until Jesus revealed it to me. I explained that Jesus was telling me these things because He wanted her to know He sees her, loves her, wants a relationship with her, and wants to heal her heart. We both ended up crying as she expressed how much this meant to her. She told me she had prayed that if Jesus was real, He would show himself to her. She told me she put a timetable on that prayer of one year. She indicated that she would not believe in God or Jesus if He did not show himself to her.

The day we met was exactly one year later, to the exact day she made her request to God. I told her Jesus is showing up for her in her time of need and wants a relationship with her so she can know His love for her. She prayed and accepted Jesus as her Lord and Savior that very night.

I was amazed she didn't have this experience sooner and felt the Lord say it was because no one was brave enough to have this conversation with her until I crossed her path. The Lord brings people into our lives for a reason. When we feel that inward witness telling us to talk to someone about Jesus, it's the Holy Spirit giving us the opportunity for someone to experience Jesus through us. We can't be inconvenienced or afraid of inconveniencing people, they were created to be connected with Jesus through a relationship. Fear shouldn't stop us from doing what the Lord tells us to do.

Street ministry doesn't have to be on a street corner with a megaphone; it can happen anywhere, at Walmart or a restaurant. It's important to be willing and ready for ministry to occur at any moment, as these personal moments can have a greater impact than group picketing for the gospel. Jesus was a fan of street ministry, as it met people where they were, with their guards down and in the midst of their daily lives. This sets a precedent for the relationship Jesus wants to have with us, that He is involved in our daily lives. That we are aware of Holy Spirit's presence in all things, and that through Him, we are being connected to the Father.

The person who is gifted in this area is a people person, outgoing, not afraid to talk to strangers. This person might have the gift of words of knowledge and be observant of people and situations around them. However, they may need help because they may talk too much and need to listen more. They may question whether they are hearing from God or not and feel like they need to make ministry happen instead of letting God direct them. They might get over-excited that God is using them and push further in a ministry conversation than the Lord was leading them. I understand this struggle. Learn how to listen and ask great questions to the second and third layer.. The best preparation for this type of ministry is to live it out of an overflowing relationship with God. Living in a relationship with God is the greatest factor in doing relational ministry.

Digital Evangelism:

Digital Evangelism is a term used to describe the use of digital technology to spread the Christian message of Jesus Christ. This includes TV the internet, social media platforms, podcasts, and eBooks and many others. With the ease of access and use of digital evangelism, it has grown significantly. One of the significant factors for this growth has been the COVID-19 pandemic, which led the church to realize the importance of being present online to meet people's needs. The easy access to digital resources has allowed evangelism to reach a larger and more diverse audience. Social media, in particular, has become a popular form of digital evangelism, allowing individuals and churches to reach and engage with many people.

People and churches can create online communities for meaningful conversations with others who have similar interests or views. Digital evangelism and social media also provide the opportunity to share Jesus's message, connecting with those seeking answers to their questions. You can become a digital missionary in today's culture without leaving your house. The ability to create and share content worldwide has always been challenging until recent advancements in social platforms. As a Christian media influencer, if you even have 30-50 people following you, which is not a lot, it's the equivalent of a small church. I currently pastor a small church, and my social media numbers are larger than the number of people that attend our church. I bring this up because it is all about perspective. Most small churches have a small reach. Any individual can have a wider reach if you can use digital influences to spread the gospel. A small church that uses digital media well in its community can do very well at reaching others for Jesus.

Don't be discouraged by small numbers. Digital creators for Christ can spread the gospel in the world. There are a number of different social media platforms you could use. At the moment of writing this, there are a lot which allow you to put the same content across multiple platforms. That being said, it is wise to learn a few platforms, see what you like best, and then focus on that platform. Once you understand that platform, you will want to grow into others. Don't get stuck on just one because social media can blacklist or shut you down. Create a connection point with your followers and get them on an email list. This information will be key if you get locked out of a social media platform.

The person who has a digital ministry gift is someone who has a bit of creativity to them. Someone who is a good communicator and can make clear points in a quick, timely manner. You might have a bent towards technology and understand the setup it takes to create – people who do well tend to be authentic and open. You might have a skill set in one or more of the areas of teaching, preaching, storytelling, and connecting. If this is an area of interest, but you feel like you lack the skillset to start, I would tell you to rip off the Band-Aid off and start. You will learn and grow along the way. You can't fear how you appear to others, or this type of ministry will eat you alive.

I look back at some of my first videos and cringe because of how bad they were. Now I have gotten so much better because I have been doing it for some time, and I try to grow from each video. One downside to this ministry is that you open yourself up to criticism from keyboard warriors. You must be secure within yourself to withstand criticism and be gracious back. It's easy to fall into the trap of wanting clicks, views, and subscribers. One may get a negative feeling when not many people see what you are producing. I struggled with this for several years. Your self-worth and identity are not in the numbers but from your relationship with Jesus. When you submit this process to the Lord, it is His to do with what he wants. The way you grow and put your hand on the plow is to learn the social media platform you are using and how the algorithm works.

Experiment with different ideas. Know the target audience you want your content to reach. Don't just say Christians or unsaved people. I have someone in mind when I make content. His name is Eric. He is married and has a father. His age range is between 28-45. He feels like there is more to life than what he is currently living and wants more out of it. I create content that Eric wants to see and watch. Digital evangelism is global. There are people in countries where they do not have access to the teachings of Jesus; the internet and social media platforms provide a way to reach them through online resources such as podcasts, blogs, websites, and eBooks. This allows for the sharing of ideas and helps those who might not have access to them in their physical community.

In conclusion, digital evangelism has become a popular and powerful way to share the gospel message of Jesus Christ. With the ease of access and reach of digital resources, individuals and churches can have a significant impact in helping people grow in their faith journey.

CHAPTER 3

Jesus was an Evangelist

When it comes to evangelism, no one did better than Jesus. I mean, come on, it helps that he is the Christ; however, he is the best example of what it means to be a risen church and live a lifestyle of evangelism. Among many of his impressive attributes, we will be breaking down his evangelistic style.

1. His Message of Redemption:

The profound message of redemption was at the heart of Jesus' evangelistic mission. His words were an invitation to people of all backgrounds or circumstances, to partake in the transformative power of God's love. In the Gospel of Matthew, Jesus encapsulates this inclusivity in the renowned Great Commission: "Go therefore and make disciples of all nations, baptizing them in the name of the Father and of the Son and of the Holy Spirit, teaching them to observe all that I have commanded you."* (Matthew 28:19-20 ESV) In these verses, we witness not only the universality of Jesus' message but also the explicit call to share it with others – a foundational aspect of effective evangelism.

2. The Art of Storytelling:

One of the distinguishing features of Jesus' evangelistic approach was his masterful use of storytelling or parables. Through these stories, he conveyed profound spiritual truths in a way that resonated with many different people. The parable of the Prodigal Son (Luke 15:11-32) stands as a testament to Jesus' storytelling brilliance, illustrating God's boundless mercy and love for all who repent. By employing relatable, everyday scenarios, Jesus broke down barriers and made the kingdom accessible to common folk through teaching them. In doing so, he demonstrated the power of storytelling by engaging hearts and minds to understand the message, and be able to share the message themselves – because they could remember the story.

3. Compassion as a Catalyst:

In most interactions, Jesus was filled with and moved by compassion for others. This is the truest nature of an evangelistic spirit. The Gospels are examples where he reached out to the forgotten, the sick, and the socially scorned. In the healing of the leper (Matthew 8:1-4), we witness a miraculous act and a powerful expression of compassion that broke societal norms. Jesus was "Moved with pity, he stretched out his hand and touched him and said to him, 'I will be clean.'"* (Mark 1:41 ESV) Jesus' compassion became a magnet, drawing individuals toward His message of hope, healing, and restoration. His actions teach aspiring evangelists the profound impact of genuine care for the well-being of others in building bridges to share the good news.

4. Personal Engagement:

Beyond the crowds and sermons, Jesus engaged with individuals on a personal level. We see this in his healing acts. Jesus demonstrated the transformative power of personal connection. "For the Son of Man came to seek and to save the lost."* (Luke 19:10 ESV). This intentional, one-on-one engagement speaks to the importance of seeing individuals beyond their circumstances, acknowledging their worth, and fostering a personal connection – a lesson resonant for the risen church evangelists seeking to impact lives on an individual level.

5. Demonstrating Authority:

In addition to words of compassion, Jesus' evangelistic Authority was manifest in his miraculous deeds. The healing of the paralytic (Mark 2:1-12) not only displayed divine power but also served as a tangible manifestation of the forgiveness of sins – a key component of Jesus' evangelistic message. "But that you may know that the Son of Man has authority on earth to forgive sins" – he said to the paralytic – 'I say to you, rise, pick up your bed, and go home.'"* (Mark 2:10-11 ESV). By intertwining words with deeds, Jesus conveyed a holistic message of salvation that spoke not only to the mind but also to the deepest needs of the heart – a profound strategy for us evangelists to consider.

6. The Cross as the Ultimate Evangelistic Act:

The pinnacle of Jesus' evangelistic mission culminated in the sacrificial act of the cross. In his encounter with Nicodemus (John 3:16), Jesus encapsulated the essence of his mission – to offer eternal life through belief in him. "For God so loved the world, that he gave his only Son, that whoever believes in him should not perish but have eternal life."* (John 3:16 ESV) The cross, as the ultimate expression of love and redemption, became the focal point of Jesus' evangelistic message. By willingly bearing the weight of humanity's sins, he provided a pathway to reconciliation with God, underscoring the profound depth of God's love for all. This is an example for us to live out as Christians. Luke 9:23, where we are told if we want to be his disciples, we are to take up our cross daily and follow him.

7. Commissioning Disciples:

Jesus, the master evangelist, did not confine the mission to himself. In a powerful display of mentorship, he equipped his disciples to carry forth the evangelistic torch. The appointment of the Twelve (Mark 3:13-19) marks a pivotal moment in which Jesus imparts authority and sends them on a mission. "And he appointed twelve (whom he also named apostles) so that they might be with him and he might send them out to preach and have authority to cast out demons."* (Mark 3:14-15 ESV) This commissioning serves as a model for us as evangelists, emphasizing the importance of equipping others to continue the work of sharing the good news. We do this by being in a relationship with others.

A Time-less Model for Evangelists:

In the intricate tapestry of Jesus' life and teachings, we find an unparalleled model for effective evangelism. Through the scriptures, we witness a multifaceted approach that incorporates inclusivity, storytelling, compassion, personal engagement, Authority, and sacrificial love. As The church seeks to impact a diverse world, the principles exemplified by Jesus serve as a timeless guide, resonating with the depths of the human soul and inviting all into the embrace of God's transformative love and salvation through Jesus Christ. In aspiring to be effective evangelists, let us draw inspiration from the One who not only proclaimed the good news but embodied it, leaving an indelible mark on the course of human history.

CHAPTER 4

Myth-Understandings

Myth-understanding is a myth a person believes or a misunderstanding of the truth that someone has. In this section of the book, we are going to look at some of the most common myth-understandings we as Christians have. We will expose the lie and replace it with the truth. In this chapter, we will explore several key misconceptions about evangelism which have, at times, hindered the active engagement of Christians in sharing their faith. By identifying these myths, we aim to dispel any doubts or reservations that may hinder individuals from fulfilling our call as the risen church and as evangelist. We will then proceed to replace these myths with the fundamental truths which can empower and inspire every believer to embrace evangelism as a vital part of their everyday life. In doing so, we will encourage a deeper understanding of the Christian mission, emphasizing that evangelism is not limited to clergy or select individuals but is a collective responsibility of all believers.

Myth-Understanding #1: *I have to be a better Christian or person before I share the Gospel.*

WRONG. Sharing the Gospel does not require living a perfect life for Christ. In fact, our brokenness can make our witness for Christ more impactful and relatable as we reach out and minister to other broken people. The belief that one must be better or cleaner before sharing the Gospel is a lie from the enemy, who accuses us of not being good enough to be loved or used by Christ. The biblical evidence of this is the story of the woman at the well, whose sin and brokenness intrigued people to come to see Jesus.

Another example is a man by the name of George Janko, a believer in Jesus Christ who cusses and parties and as of this writing is not living in a holy union, but still talks about Jesus as he is continuing to be transformed by his relationship with Jesus. There is fruit and evidence of this in his life in Christ. One of his best friends, who hosts one of the largest podcasts and YouTube channels, is a platform where George has occasionally talked about Jesus to his friends, guests, and audiences, often getting ridiculed by his friends for his belief in Jesus. What I love about George is that he knows he struggles with sin and admits it all the while pointing to Jesus explaining how he needs more of Jesus to be transformed into his image. I would rather see someone confess their sin versus try to hide it. Hiding one's sin is far unhealthier. George sense has gone on to create his own show and seems to be doing well as it and I see the Lord convicting him of sin and continuing to be transformed by his relationship with Jesus.

You don't have to be perfect before you start sharing the Gospel. Another part of this myth stems from the church, which has placed too much emphasis on attaining a certain level of holiness. I agree we are all called to be holy as He is holy 1 Peter 1:15-16 while the transformation of a relationship with Jesus is important. A process in the Christian life, there has been a focus on self-rightness and works. His love is the work of grace in which we are transformed into his image, not self-righteousness and doing good deeds. Out of love that has transformed us into His image, we are called to do good deeds, not good deeds to be righteous.

We should rest in Christ and allow that work to transform us into his likeness in our hearts, minds, and lifestyles.

Understanding that we live our Christian walk based on where we are and that his love, grace, and kindness lead us to repentance. (Writers side note: The word rest was not originally there. I had the word strive. I realized even at this moment; striving would be a transgression and a work of the flesh. Sometimes, God calls us to cease striving and rest more in his presence.) Does that mean we get stuck where we are? Absolutely not. The grace of Jesus Christ allows us to be transformed from our past into his image. We should start seeing our past and our future selves as being in Christ. When we live with the mindset of being identified with Christ in our future self, we live from the future into our present rather than our past. When we live from the future to the present, we tend to identify with our future and make decisions based on that belief. Paul lived from the grace given to him and that his future self was in

71

Christ through death, which he preferred. NIV Philippians 1: 20 I eagerly expect and hope that I will in no way be ashamed, but will have sufficient courage so that now as always Christ will be exalted in my body, whether by life or by death. 21For to me, to live is Christ and to die is gain. 22 If I am to go on living in the body, this will mean fruitful labor for me. Yet what shall I choose? I do not know! 23 I am torn between the two: I desire to depart and be with Christ, which is better by far; 24 but it is more necessary for you that I remain in the body. 25 Convinced of this, I know that I will remain, and I will continue with all of you for your progress and joy in the faith, 26 so that through my being with you again your boasting in Christ Jesus will abound on account of me.

When we live from the grace of Jesus that has come and is coming, we can live from our future transformed self because we are living from the grace already given both for the forgiveness of our sin and from his power to be transformed into his image.

In the NIV translation, John 1:16 reads, "Out of his fullness, we have all received grace in place of grace already given". This verse encapsulates a profound truth about the nature of Jesus and His boundless grace. It signifies that the fullness of Jesus, His divine nature and character, serves as an unending wellspring of grace for humanity. This grace, received by believers, is not a one-time gift but a continual outpouring. **"Out of his fullness" reminds us that Jesus, being the Son of God, possesses an abundance of grace that knows no limits. His grace is not finite or depleted; it is an eternal and unceasing flow.** Every believer has the privilege of drawing from this endless well of grace. "We have all received grace" signifies that this gift is not exclusive to a select few but is extended to all who come to Jesus with a repentant heart and faith in him. Our universal offer to him is that we give up our lives and make him Lord of our lives. "In place of grace already given" underscores the concept of grace upon grace. As we receive grace from Jesus, it doesn't diminish the grace already given but adds to it. It's a cumulative process, where each act of grace builds upon the previous one. This reflects God's continual, unfailing love and favor towards His children.

John 1:16 reminds us that Jesus' fullness is an infinite source of grace, accessible to all believers. This grace is not a one-time gift but an ongoing, accumulative outpouring, reflecting the boundless love and generosity of our Savior.

Paul writes in Epiphanies 2:8-9 NIV 8 "For it is by grace you have been saved, through faith – and this is not from yourselves, it is the gift of God – not by works so that no one can boast." The Best example we can be to others is to allow others to see our journey of transformation into Christ's likeness, not by our own works but by a relationship with him from his grace. If we wait until we are quote-unquote arrived before we share the Gospel, we missed the greatest opportunity for people to join us in our brokenness and journey of transformation. Jesus and his message was [and is] attractive to many because of this principle. People saw the lives of others be transformed by Jesus. This is what drew more and more people to Him. Evidence of the transformation seen in the people around them led others to hear about all the things Jesus was [and is] doing. Regardless of where you are in your walk with the Lord, we are all called to live a life that exemplifies Christ in our actions, love, and communication. This work of grace in our lives is a **living witness** of the Love and Gospel of Jesus Christ. The more we are transformed the more the more our lifestyle represent his nature.

Regarding the fear of sharing the Gospel, you might not want your lifestyle to change – you might want to hide out in your sin. Being outspoken about Jesus and salvation and his transforming power might require you to change when you don't want to. You might want to live a lifestyle of sin while you have yet to experience the transformation. If this is you, I want you to hear my heart. **I want you to rise up and take your place as the person who God is calling into his image. To let the past go and to focus on worshiping Jesus.** You don't want to be half in on Jesus. You are in, or you're out, but pick a stance. This does not mean you will be perfect; this means you will pursue a life of being transformed by God and recognize sin as sin and go to God when you sin and thank him for his grace, and to be transformed into his likeness. Shine a light on your sin, don't hide it. But when you make it public, do so wisely and with a few trusted people.

Myth Understanding 2: evangelism is wrong:

Many Christians, especially the younger millennial Christians, believe it is wrong to talk about Christ to others. They tend to believe evangelism is forcing one's beliefs on the other person, also known as being too pushy. Here is what the Barna research group has to say. *"Almost all practicing Christians believe that part of their faith means being a witness about Jesus (ranging from 95% to 97% among all generational groups) and that the best thing that could ever happen to someone is for them to know Jesus (94% to 97%). Millennials, in particular, feel equipped to share their faith with others. For instance, almost three-quarters say they know how to respond when someone raises questions about faith (73%), and that they are gifted at sharing their faith with other people (73%). This is higher than any other generational group: Gen X (66%), Boomers (59%) and Elders (56%). Despite this, many Millennials are unsure about the actual practice of evangelism. Almost half of Millennials (47%) agree at least somewhat that it is wrong to share one's personal beliefs with someone of a different faith in hopes that they will one day share the same faith. This is compared to a little over one-quarter of Gen X (27%), and one in five Boomers (19%) and Elders (20%). (Though Gen Z teens were not included in this study, their thoroughly post-Christian posture will likely amplify this stance toward evangelism.) https://www. barna.com/research/millennials-oppose-evangelism/*

What is the cause of 47% of younger Christians (Millennials) believing that sharing their faith is wrong? It is believed the sensitivity of people today and the fear of offending others is the main cause. This culture values individual truth over actual truth, and when confronted with the truth, some become easily offended. Barna wrote a book called "Spiritual Conversations in a Digital Age." Despite others being easily offended, it is not wrong for Christians to do evangelism. We cannot control the emotional intelligence of others. If someone is offended by our beliefs, that is their issue as long as we speak the truth in love. We cannot let the actions or responses of others prevent us from fulfilling what God has called us to do through a lifestyle of evangelism. This is often seen in scripture, where people are offended by the truth because it confronts their sin and lifestyle.

(NLT) 1 Corinthians 1: 18 The message of the cross is foolish to those who are headed for destruction! But we who are being saved know it is the very power of God. (NLT) Isaiah 8:14-16 But to Israel and Judah, he will be a stone that makes people stumble, a rock that makes them fall. And for the people of Jerusalem, he will be a trap and a snare. 15 Many will stumble and fall, never to rise again. They will be snared and captured." 16 Preserve the teaching of God; entrust his instructions to those who follow me. (NLT) 1 Peter 2:8: "He is the stone that makes people stumble, the rock that makes them fall."

From the beginning of time, living a life unto God and in his grace for a holy life has always been offensive because it requires us to put down our selfishness and our own ambitions and even go against culture and submit to the Lord for his plan and lifestyle in our lives. This is what makes him the Lord of our life, not just our savior, for fire insurance purposes. People are not more offended by the Gospel today than 2000 years ago. The same spirit of offense then is the same spirit of offense we see in our world today. The difference is in our society, we have made those who are easily offended victims. And because they are victims the leading ideology in our culture tells us that means the offended has the moral high ground. This is such a lie and could not be further from the truth. Christians who are afraid to offend someone with the truth have become fearful, thus weakening the church and our understanding and belief in the spiritual power and authority we have in Jesus. This is because the church forgot it is a risen church, not a dead church. Christianity in our culture has been watered down, and people nowadays do not know what it means to live in the power of the baptism of the holy spirit, and be indwelled by this second work of grace. Matthew 28:18-20 ESV And Jesus came and said to them, "All authority in heaven and on earth has been given to me. Go therefore and make disciples of all nations, baptizing them in the name of the father and of the son and of the Holy Spirit, teaching them to observe all that I have commanded you. And behold, I am with you always, to the end of the age."

It's as if our culture and outlook have turned Christianity into just another worldview or religion, but Jesus says in John 14:6, "I am the way, the truth, and the life. No one can come to the father except through me." As Christians, we need to live from the power of being the risen church which comes from the Holy Spirit, and not fear the perceived offense someone may take. We should live bold and courageous lives, declaring salvation through faith and the Lordship of Jesus Christ that we are united with the father because of the death, barrel, and resurrection of Jesus Christ. As a church culture, we have been aggressively pursuing comfort in our lives for a long time. It has weakened the church to take a stand against adversity. Why? Because it is uncomfortable.

(Authors Side note – do things that make you uncomfortable. Take a cold shower and exercise; we are created to do hard things.) Practicing the discipline of doing hard things makes it easier to do other things that may or may not be in our control. Doing hard things makes it easier to share the gospel of Jesus Christ. One of my mentors, Matt Olsen, taught me this in college, **"great men do the things they don't want to do when they don't want to do them."** This has been a guiding principle in my life and has helped me take action in many areas where I otherwise would not have.

'If someone gets offended when you share Jesus with them, you should be led by God and seek His guidance. If you're unsure of what to do, you can end the conversation and thank them for letting you share. Alternatively, you can become bolder and pursue a spiritual moment in the hope that their heart opens to the truth. Sometimes this works well, and sometimes it does not. Ultimately, do not let the spirit of fear overcome you when someone gets offended. You are responsible for telling the truth in love, but how others receive it is up to them. Christians have walked on eggshells in America because we do not want to offend people. Still, the truth is that people who get offended are everywhere. Even if you don't share the Gospel, they are looking for something else to be offended by. So they might as well be offended by the truth in love.

Throughout history, there have been stories of how evangelism has changed nations. The movie "End of the Spear" is based on a story about five missionary families who traveled to Eastern Ecuador to evangelize the

Huaorani (Waodani) people. Although the five missionary men were killed, the remaining wives and children carried on their vision. They lived among the tribe and led them to know Jesus Christ. This story not only changed the tribe but affected others who watched the movie.

Evangelism is a vital and powerful tool for advancing the kingdom of God against the kingdom of darkness. We have countless examples of individuals willing to sacrifice their lives for Christ. We should not fear other people's opinions, how they will view us, or the chance of being canceled. Sharing the Gospel can profoundly impact individuals, families, and even entire cities, even if it takes time for the seed of evangelism to grow in people's hearts.

In America, the church has become soft. Because we have aggressively pursued comfort, neglecting the discomfort of carrying our cross. We have been blessed not to know what life or death persecution is like in most other countries. We have not had to risk losing our lives fighting for religious freedoms from a tyrannical, oppressive government or dictator in quite some time. However this page is beginning to turn, and if we are not ready for the discomfort of that situation, we will be led astray. If as Christians we are weak we won't even show up for the spiritual fight of our lives or the lives of others around us.

The life we live is a spiritual battleground and it's important to recognize that. Pretending that it is not doesn't help you. We are like the Israelite army scared when Goliath taunted them for 30 days. We need to have the same spirit and confidence David had in God. Because of this he turned the culture around – from a spirit of fear to

79

confidence in the Lord. This happened because David did not start off fighting the giant. He started off with a lion and a bear. We have many lions and bears in our lives. Let those be the building blocks of hardship and discomfort to have faith in God to share the Gospel of salvation.

3rd Myth-Understanding: There is a common misconception that we can live as good Christians, and others will automatically come to know God.

This idea needs to be revised. While being a good example is important, we must also use our words to preach the Gospel unless God tells us otherwise. The idea that all we need to do is live by example for others to develop a relationship with God is a myth. The idea that we do not need to use words to preach the Gospel is wrong. Yes, be a good example to grow in Christ and Christian virtues but use words so people have understanding and belief.

It is said that actions speak louder than words. Words are the architect of our actions. Thoughts or words take place in our heads before actions take place. A quote by Francis of Assisi reads, "Preach the gospel at all times, and if necessary, use words." The myth behind this statement is that all it takes for people to understand the Gospel is to be a good example. While it is important to live a life that embodies Christ in front of others and in private, relying solely on this is not enough. We are commanded in the Bible to go into all the world and preach the Gospel, which requires us to use our words. The Greek word used in the New Testament for "preach" is "κηρύσσω" (pronounced "kay-roos'-so"), which means to proclaim, announce, or herald a message publicly. It specifically refers to the act of proclaiming or preaching the good news of the Gospel. This word is often used in the context of sharing the message of salvation and calling people to repentance and faith in Jesus Christ.

Often, Christians struggle to find the balance between living as an example and using their words to preach the Gospel. Some may talk about their faith, but their actions do not align with their words, while others may live as good examples but never communicate their beliefs. The key is to do both. Like a teacher who teaches and exemplifies what they want their students to learn, we must live in pursuit of acting differently than the world. As Christians, we need to explain to others why Jesus is Lord and how he transforms us into his likeness from a life of sin.

The story of Philip and the Ethiopian eunuch in Acts 8:26-40 is a great example of the importance of using words to preach the Gospel. In this story, Philip used his words to explain the Gospel to the Ethiopian eunuch and led him to his understanding of Jesus' work on the cross. Colossians 3:17 instructs us to do everything, whether in word or deed, in the name of the Lord Jesus, giving thanks to God the Father through him. People should know us as Christians by the way we speak and live. Still, it is also necessary to use words to explain our beliefs so that people may understand what they see so that they, too, may believe.

People may refrain from using words to share the Gospel due to fear, such as feeling inadequate or concerned about what others may think. This fear can stem from inward thoughts about oneself that they don't know enough. This can be overcome through prayer, fasting, and biblical studying and counseling with a professional or a pastor. Some may fear being seen as a hypocrite – it is important to remember we are all imperfect. The best witness is someone who is pointing towards Jesus and sharing their need for Him, even amid their struggles.

God plans to save people, and sharing the truth about salvation with others is not judgmental. There is a common misconception that talking about Jesus is judgmental, but this is often based on fear and the idea that everyone has their own truth. The truth is that there is only one standard of truth and sharing it in love is not judgmental. It is important to remember that people will eventually be judged based on their actions or the work of Jesus on the cross. When sharing the Gospel, it is helpful to approach it from a relatable perspective. Sharing your personal story of how you needed salvation can help the other person understand that you are not trying to condemn them but instead offer them the gift of salvation. If someone reacts negatively to the Gospel, it may be a spiritual issue they are dealing with rather than a personal offense towards you. Despite the potential discomfort, it is important not to let fear keep you from sharing the truth in love with those who need it.

Myth – understanding 4: Many people believe that only ordained ministers or those with professional training can do evangelism.

This is a myth. When Jesus was ascending into heaven, he told the crowd to go and preach the Gospel, and none of them were ordained. Most of the five hundred people present were not his disciples; many had never shared the Gospel. You are in good company to share the Gospel. It's understandable to feel nervous about sharing your faith because of a lack of confidence or knowledge of the Bible or the teachings of Jesus. However, you do not have to have all the answers. What's most important is that you share your faith with honesty and sincerity and as much biblical accuracy as you have knowledge of and be willing to learn and grow in your understanding of the Bible.

Rejection is a common experience which can be hurtful. For many people, past trauma from rejection keeps them from sharing the message of salvation. It's understandable to feel intimidated by the prospect of sharing your beliefs and being rejected or ridiculed. However, it's important to remember everyone has the right to make their own choices, and not everyone will choose to follow Jesus. It's not your responsibility if they don't. What's most important is that you were brave enough to share the Gospel, even when it was difficult.

Ordination is not a requirement for evangelism. Your desire to see others come to Christ is more important than a piece of paper. A pastor once shared with his audience that they didn't need a certification to be witnesses of the Gospel. He gave everyone a certificate that certified them to preach the Gospel in Jesus' name. This is a powerful reminder that anyone can share the Gospel and spread the message of Jesus, regardless of their knowledge, skills, or training. All that's required is a sincere desire to share the love of Jesus with others and see the kingdom of God advance.

Myth-Understanding 5: We cannot talk about hell when sharing the Gospel.

Over the years, I have experienced and heard of many reasons why people may be afraid to talk about hell when sharing the Gospel. The fear of offending others: Some Christians may be afraid of offending non-believers by talking about hell. You may worry that mentioning hell will turn others off of the salvation message or make them feel uncomfortable. If we truly love all people, we, at times, have to risk people being offended by the truth. Remember, the Bible tells us the Gospel is offensive. If we are not willing to tell the truth in love, then we are living out of fear – for fear – of being offensive. I ask you, friends, to not witness out of a spirit of fear but witness according to 2 Timothy 1:7, "For God hath not given us the spirit of fear; but of power, and of love, and of a sound mind." (KJB).

When talking about hell, we do not solely preach from a megaphone, "Repent you, sinner, you are going to hell." Yeah, that would be a turn-off. This is not the kind of evangelism I am talking about. When discussing hell, the best thing to say is that Christ has given us salvation to spend eternity with him and free us from his wrath, and hell if we accept his gift of salvation. The sin and rejection of salvation is our choice. God does not send us to hell; it is our choices and actions that do.

I have found that many Christians lack an understanding of some of the concepts of hell. This may be a reason Christians are afraid to bring it up. They are afraid of questions they don't have answers to (more on objection handling later). Some may be afraid to talk about hell because they do not feel confident in their own beliefs or understanding of the topic. They may worry they will not be able to articulate their thoughts effectively or will be challenged or questioned by others. It's hard talking about something you don't feel confident in, but the more conversations you have about that topic, the better you become and the more confidence you will have. Practicing hard conversations with people outside of just witnessing will help you develop your ability to witness.

We, the church, need to educate ourselves on common questions people have about the Lord and be able to answer them, not only for them but for our own understanding and personal relationship with God. This will help us stand firm in times of doubt. We have always been told that there are two subjects you never talk about at work – politics, and religion. Why, because of personal discomfort? Avoiding discomfort leads to weakness. As well as avoiding offending others, the topic of hell can be very unpleasant. Some people may feel uncomfortable talking about hell because they find the topic disturbing or unpleasant because the idea of burning forever in a lake of fire does not sound like fun.

It's morbid, really. They may not want to think about the possibility of hell or about the suffering that could take place there. I find this is often like death. We all know we will die someday, but not very many people want to think about it. It's why so many people don't have life insurance a trust or will. They don't want to face the reality of death, and the pain of thinking about it is uncomfortable. Just like the idea of death makes us think about our mortality. Thinking about hell confronts people about being a sinner – which is why it is important that you ask them if they die today where they are going, Heaven or hell. **People go to hell because they reject God, not God rejecting them.**

Myth-Understanding 6: People will always respond poorly to sharing your faith.

This is just that – a myth. Only about 50% of people will react badly, so you got a 50/50 shot. In reality, people's response depends on two things. How you set the conversation up, how loving you come across, and the level of offense and hurt that person carries around with them towards Christianity. In my experience, people respond differently to conversations based on my style of evangelism. Street evangelism or public evangelism may result in more negative responses, but that is only the case for some discussions or types of evangelism. People are more open to evangelism through conversation than you think. Don't let fear of a poor experience stop you from doing what God calls upon you. Sharing the Gospel has positive results but is often ignored and sometimes negative. I find people far more open when I ask them how to pray for them first. Still, it is essential to know how to respond to negative ones.

You may be afraid of a poor response because you are unsure what to say or how to start the conversation. It's okay if you don't have all the answers to tough questions. The Holy Spirit does, and you can ask for guidance in real time. When I am open about not knowing everything, I often gain more respect from the person I am talking to, as it shows them that I am willing to learn. Even if I can't answer the tricky question, I respond with I don't know, but I'll get back to you on that topic, and the conversation usually continues.

It's normal to feel discouraged after a bad experience, but the more you share the Gospel, the more confident you will become. Over time and through practice, your beliefs about yourself and your identity will be shaped, and you will start to see yourself as a witness for the Gospel. You will also have more success stories which become the foundation of encouragement for your future. Don't stop when it's hard; it will get easier with time. Remember your vision for yourself and your family can transform your identity and how you view yourself. When I started walking 5ks, my desire to become an active and fit family. That process has transformed my identity in an area of my life.

l My identity prior to being more active was one that was not healthy. I ate poorly; I was not active. Putting myself through the process of training, learning, and growing in my health and fitness was and is still hard. It hurts mentally and physically. Over the past few years, I have lost over 40 lbs. My identity started being shaped by the experience of being healthy, not the pain that it took to get there. **Pain shaped my ability to learn endurance in the midst of adversity. Endurance has built my character and character created hope in the midst of adversity. Do you see the repeating pattern?**

Now, I am more accustomed to the pain. I have built a tolerance to it, and my workout is more effective. **My identity has transformed to being able to do hard things. Not off of the results I have seen, but who I become through the process.** Evangelism is the same way. It will be hard, uncomfortable, and might even hurt at first. As you gain a few successes in witnessing, it becomes more encouraging. Your identity about yourself in evangelism starts being transformed as you see successful results and go through the process.

Myth-Understanding 7: I don't know enough to be sharing the Gospel:

Many people believe they need to have a deep understanding of the Bible and be able to answer every question before they can share the Gospel effectively. This can make sharing the Gospel seem daunting and unachievable. However, it is essential to remember that a deep understanding of the Bible is not necessary to be a witness for Jesus. Jesus commanded the man He healed in Luke 8:38-39 to go back to his family and tell them everything God had done for him. Jesus did not require the man to follow Him to the synagogues to memorize the Old Testament. Instead, the man had everything he needed to share the Gospel; his encounter with Jesus.

The key to sharing the Gospel is regularly encountering Jesus and sharing your testimony and knowledge of him and the scripture with others. You do not have to be a biblical scholar to be a witness for Jesus. All that is needed is your willingness to share the love and Gospel of Jesus, regardless of your abilities and understanding. While biblical knowledge and understanding are always encouraged, there is no particular level of experience one must have before they start sharing the Gospel. Trust in God's ability and not your own when witnessing, as God goes before you and will come behind you.

Studying the promises and assurances of the Bible can be helpful in bringing comfort and hope to others who are in need, but it is not a requirement for sharing the Gospel. God can use anyone, regardless of their abilities, to share the Gospel. As it says in Numbers 22, God even used a donkey to talk to Balaam. So if God can use an ass to speak, he can use you and me. I think most of us can be equivalent or greater than an ass. Pun intended.

My father-in-law Paul, who is mostly bedridden, still evangelizes to people almost daily. When telemarketers call the house, he tells them that he will listen to them if they listen to him first. He will start sharing the gospel. At this moment, one of two things happens. They hang up, # win because you don't have to talk to them anymore, or they listen and hear the gospel. That is also a win.

I do a ministry in the fall through a free prayer booth I created at the Tulsa State Fair. I partnered with other evangelistic ministries and together, we had over 350 volunteers over 11 days, and 479 people gave their lives to Jesus. We had people show up to help from all over the United States because they wanted to share the Gospel. Towards the event's beginning, a father and son came from Colorado. The father was there to help, and his 19-year-old son, who was severely autistic, was tagging along. On the first day, the autistic son just watched people evangelize to others. On the second day, I worked with him for a bit and encouraged him to take the microphone and preach as people were going by. He did not have a great depth of understanding of biblical principles. Still, he had a voice and an understanding of Jesus' love for people. So for an hour, he said Jesus loves you as people walked by. Then he started talking about forgiveness very simply, saying that God forgives you. This young man's name is Elijah. I did not know him well, and that was the first time interacting with him.

Later that day, his father came to me crying about seeing his son being given an opportunity to preach. He said, "I never thought something like this would be available for him. I did not think my son would even do something like this. He was so grateful his son was given an opportunity to witness to other people. His son was timid and not generally open to people, let alone a public crowd with a lot of activity and noise. To see that happen was a miracle.

I firmly believe all you need to do is be a willing vessel to share the love of Jesus Christ with others. God will use what you have to offer him much as he did when he fed 5000 from five loaves of bread and two fish a boy gave as an offering – it was Jesus' job to multiply what was given to feed the masses. **So many times, we think we are the multiplication factor in ministry, but we are not. Its Jesus and the Holy Spirit.** We are the boys and girls who give what little we have.

CHAPTER 5

Difficult conversation-Scripting

Navigating difficult conversations is essential in practicing lifestyle evangelism, where our actions and behavior reflect our faith. Various obstacles can arise that make these conversations challenging. Here are some strategies for overcoming these obstacles and effectively engaging in discussions about faith. Starting a difficult conversation with empathy is crucial because it acknowledges the uniqueness of each individual's perspective and experiences. Recognizing that people may have different beliefs, values, or backgrounds helps us approach conversations with an open mind and heart. Empathy allows us to set aside preconceived notions or biases and genuinely listen to the other person's viewpoint without judgment or criticism.

Approaching conversations with empathy creates a space for dialogue. When individuals feel understood and respected, they are more likely to express their thoughts and feelings honestly. Creating this environment encourages open and honest communication, where both parties can freely share their perspectives, concerns, and doubts. This allows for a deeper exploration of ideas and fosters a sense of trust and mutual respect.

Empathy is a powerful tool for building bridges between differing viewpoints. When we seek to understand someone's perspective, we demonstrate our willingness to validate their experiences and emotions. This empathetic approach helps break down barriers and facilitates a connection based on shared beliefs. It paves the way for meaningful conversations where both parties can learn from one another, challenge their assumptions, and grow in understanding. Ultimately, starting with empathy sets the tone for constructive dialogue and lays the foundation for building stronger relationships, even in the midst of difficult conversations.

Respectful communication is essential in navigating difficult conversations as it sets the tone for a constructive and meaningful dialogue. Speaking with kindness, gentleness, and humility creates an atmosphere of mutual respect and openness. When we approach conversations with respect, we acknowledge the inherent worth and dignity of the other person, fostering a safe space where ideas can be freely shared and explored.

Knowing your audience is a key factor in effective communication, especially when navigating difficult conversations. Adapting your approach based on the individuals or groups you are engaging with allows you to connect on a deeper level and foster understanding. By taking the time to understand or think through their background, beliefs, and cultural context, you can tailor your language, examples, and overall communication style to resonate with their experiences, making the conversation more relatable and meaningful.

Understanding your audience's background helps you approach the conversation with sensitivity and respect. It enables you to appreciate their unique perspectives, values, and traditions. By recognizing and acknowledging their beliefs and cultural context, you create a space that honors their identity and fosters a sense of inclusivity. This understanding allows you to choose your words carefully, avoiding language or examples that may inadvertently cause offense or misunderstanding. Instead, you can select references or analogies that are more likely to resonate with their experiences, making the conversation relatable and engaging.

Tailoring your communication to your audience enhances the effectiveness of your message. You can do this without diluting the truth of the gospel. When you speak in a way that aligns with their worldview or experiences, it increases the chances of them truly understanding and connecting with what you are conveying. By using language and examples that are familiar to them, you can bridge potential gaps in understanding and foster a sense of shared understanding. This tailored approach also shows that you have taken the time and effort to understand their perspective, which can strengthen trust and credibility.

Ultimately, knowing your audience allows you to meet them where they are and create a space for genuine dialogue. It demonstrates your respect for their individuality and affirms their worth as participants in the conversation. By adapting your approach and tailoring your communication, you create an openness to where perspectives can be shared and understood. This is important because if you give space to someone to speak freely, then through reciprocity, they should offer you the same opportunity. This enriches the conversation and creates an opportunity for mutual growth, learning, and, ultimately, a deeper connection.

I drove with a friend to pick up dinner for our family hangout. I was talking to him about Jesus and Christianity. He was willing to be open and vulnerable with me. He said Evan, you know why I can't believe in Jesus? I said tell me. He said I believe in aliens, and Christians don't believe in aliens. I thanked him for feeling like he could trust me with that information. I leaned in and said can I tell you something, he said yes. I said I believe in Jesus, and I believe in aliens. He said, you do, I said yes, just not in the same way. You believe in extraterrestrials as aliens, correct? Yes, he said, well, I believe in aliens, not as extraterrestrials but as intra-terrestrials. I used the multiverse from Marvel as an example. I said I believe there are aliens that can move through different dimensions and have the ability to shape-shift and pretend to be other beings or take possession of other people if allowed. My views intrigued him; he said he never thought of it that way. I was describing different spiritual dimensions we cannot see in our physical body. I told him what he believes are aliens I believe are demons. I took it one step further, wanting to talk to him on his level. I told him what people think might come in a so-called alien abduction will actually be the rapture of Christians to Jesus Christ.

You see I was able to talk to him about biblical principles from a place of his own understanding. This opens the door for me to talk about Jesus coming from a perspective he believed in. Avoiding defensiveness or confrontational behavior is key to maintaining respectful communication. When we become defensive, we tend to shut down the conversation or engage in personal attacks, hindering any potential for understanding or growth. Instead, remaining calm and composed allows us to listen attentively and respond thoughtfully. It demonstrates our willingness to engage in a constructive exchange of ideas rather than seeking to prove ourselves right or undermine the other person's perspective.

Using "I" statements to express our beliefs and experiences is another important aspect of respectful communication. By framing our thoughts in terms of personal experiences or beliefs, we avoid imposing our viewpoints on others. This approach allows for a more open and non-threatening conversation, inviting the other person to share their thoughts and perspectives without feeling attacked or judged. It promotes active listening and encourages a genuine exchange of ideas where both parties can learn from each other's unique perspectives.

Respectful communication fosters an open exchange of ideas. When we approach conversations with respect, we create an environment where individuals feel valued and heard. This encourages them to share their thoughts and opinions openly, without fear of ridicule or dismissal.

Respectful communication allows for the exploration of differing viewpoints, providing an opportunity for personal growth, and expanding our understanding of the world. It builds bridges between individuals with different perspectives, enabling us to find common ground and work towards mutual understanding and reconciliation.

Through my journey in counseling, I have come to a profound realization about myself: I have a tendency to dismiss other people's thoughts and feelings, particularly when their opinions or viewpoints differ from my own. I now understand that this behavior stems from an internal issue, a deep-seated wound that I am actively working on addressing. It's as if I perceive any differing perspective as a personal attack on me, leading me to invalidate the experiences and emotions of those around me. This new-found awareness has been a pivotal moment of growth and self-discovery. As I delve into the depths of my trauma and wounds, I am learning the importance of compassion, empathy, and genuine understanding. I've come to realize that when I feel attacked, it's crucial not to let that emotional response cloud my judgment or overshadow the value of someone else's experiences .

I am a work in progress on this matter. In the process of sharing the gospel and reaching out to others, this lesson holds immense significance. I can become a more effective and empathetic communicator by recognizing and removing my personal triggers from the equation. I now understand that the real enemy, the adversary, can exploit our triggers during evangelism, hindering the power of our witness. Through this journey of healing and being transformed into Christ's image, I have grown in my faith and deepened my understanding of the gospel's true essence. This is to know God, experience his love and be transformed by it, then share it with others so they may know Him. I've learned that opening my heart to others' stories allows me to embrace the experiences of others and the unique design that God made that person to be.

If I listen to what they are saying, it shows them that I am willing to accept them. It has also made me realize that each individual's journey is unique which allows me to connect with people in ways Christians may not have in the past. Does this mean we accept and love sin? No, I love them despite their sin and hope that they encounter Jesus; and through that, they are transformed into his image.

In conclusion, my experience in counseling has been a transformative process. I've learned to be more openminded, empathetic, and understanding, which has enriched my relationships and strengthened my faith. As I continue to work on addressing my internal struggles, I am becoming better equipped to share the gospel with love, humility, and a genuine desire to connect with others versus thinking what I believe is right. They need to believe in it because I am right. The realization that my personal healing journey can positively impact my ability to witness to others fills me with hope and gratitude.

It is crucial for us, as Christians, to remember that acknowledging someone's humanity and worth does not equate to validating their sin. As followers of Christ our foundation should always be rooted in biblical truth. We recognize every individual as a creation of God, uniquely and purposefully made, and deeply loved by Him. In our approach to evangelism, this awareness becomes the bedrock upon which we stand. By seeing others through the lens of God's love and recognizing their intrinsic value as His creation, we can mirror the likeness of Christ in our interactions. It means embracing a perspective of compassion, understanding, and empathy, just as Hebrews 4:15 reminds us: "For we do not have a high priest who is unable to empathize with our weaknesses, but we have one who has been tempted in every way, just as we are – yet he did not sin." (Hebrews 4:15, NIV)

Asking open-ended questions is a powerful tool for navigating difficult conversations, especially when discussing faith-related topics. Open-ended questions invite the other person to reflect and share their thoughts meaningfully. By posing questions that require more than a simple yes or no answer, we encourage deeper exploration and provide space for the other person to express their ideas and beliefs.

Open-ended questions also demonstrate a genuine interest in the other person's perspective. When we ask thoughtful and open-ended questions, we show that we value their thoughts and experiences. This approach creates an environment where the other person feels heard and respected, fostering a sense of trust and openness. It encourages them to engage more actively in the conversation making it richer and more meaningful.

Furthermore, open-ended questions allow for a broader exploration of faith-related topics. By encouraging the other person to reflect and elaborate on their beliefs, we create an opportunity for them to delve deeper into their own thoughts. This exploration can lead to a better understanding of their worldview, enabling us to find points of connection and areas for further discussion as well as the ability for them to find flaws in their own perspective. Open-ended questions promote critical thinking and self-reflection, ultimately enhancing the quality of the conversation and fostering a deeper understanding of one another and the overall topic.

When you don't ask open-ended questions in a conversation, it can limit the depth and quality of the discussion. Closed-ended questions, which can be answered with a simple "yes" or "no" or a brief response, often restrict the opportunity for the other person to express their thoughts and engage in meaningful dialogue. This can lead to a superficial exchange of information without truly exploring the underlying beliefs, values, or experiences related to the topic at hand. In addition, without open-ended questions, the conversation may become one-sided, with one person dominating the discussion or simply providing brief responses. This can create a power imbalance and hinder the development of a genuine connection and understanding between individuals. It may also prevent the exploration of different perspectives and hinder the discovery of common ground or shared understanding. Without the opportunity to delve deeper and reflect on their own beliefs and experiences, the other person may feel unheard or dismissed, leading to a breakdown in communication and a missed opportunity for growth and mutual understanding.

The reason why open-ended questions are so important is that they breathe life into conversations. As a real estate agent, I have experienced the profound impact of using open-ended questions during my cold calls for sale by owners and expired listings. In the initial years of cold calling, I found myself trapped in a cycle of asking questions that only garnered yes or no answers. Consequently, I struggled to build meaningful conversations that could benefit both the homeowners and me. Realizing the need for change, I decided to revamp my script entirely.

Instead of bombarding potential clients with inquiries like, "Is this Mr. Jones?" or "Do you live at 123 Main Street?" or "Are you still interested in selling your home? or "Are you looking for a new real estate agent? " I adopted a more engaging approach. I began assuming I was speaking to Mr. Jones at 123 Main Street and crafted my introduction accordingly. This shift in tone allowed me to ask more thought-provoking questions, like "If your home had sold, where were you planning to move to?" What did you like or dislike about your last experience? What would you want your next real estate agent to do?"

By framing my questions in an open-ended manner, I encouraged homeowners to delve deeper into their thoughts and feelings. Often, this led to responses where they freely shared this information with me, allowing me to know what was most important to them. It showed me their experiences and why they view their situation, the way they do. These genuine questions were the catalyst for building rapport and understanding each individual's unique needs and desires. This allowed me to share information and my presentation with them in a manner that was best for them to be willing to listen and receive it.

In the process of evangelism, effective communication is vital. Just as with my real estate calls, I've learned that understanding how to guide a conversation can be a powerful tool without manipulating the other person. As representatives sharing the love and peace of God through evangelism, it is our responsibility to create a comfortable environment for others to express themselves freely, even if they are initially defensive. Not being combative or defensive myself and asking open-ended questions allows them to let down the walls they built to guard themselves, which is a self-preservation mechanism. If I went into sales mode, the walls would be up, and they would feel like I am imposing on them.

Rather than imposing our beliefs on others, we aim to guide the conversation in a way that addresses their concerns, doubts, and desires. Just as homeowners may want to sell their homes but may not know how to articulate it, people seeking spiritual fulfillment may yearn for God's love and salvation but struggle to express it clearly or understand why they need it because they are in self-preservation mode. By attentively listening and understanding what matters most to them, we can respond with empathy and compassion, providing insights and guidance while respecting their individual journey.

In conclusion, open-ended questions are essential tools in building connections, whether in the realm of real estate or evangelism. They open doors to meaningful conversations, fostering trust, understanding, and mutual respect.

As we engage with others, we are privileged to steer conversations with care, allowing them to express their hearts' desires while we share the transformative power of God's love and grace. The art of communication in both professions lies in the ability to connect with people authentically, acknowledging their needs and desires, and offering genuine support and guidance along the way.

Addressing misconceptions is an important aspect of navigating difficult conversations. Misconceptions or stereotypes about faith can hinder open and meaningful dialogue. Being prepared to address these misconceptions enables us to provide accurate information and gently correct any misunderstandings that may arise. Doing so establishes a foundation of trust and credibility, fostering an environment conducive to a more informed and productive discussion.

When addressing misconceptions, it is essential to provide accurate information. This may involve sharing relevant facts, citing credible sources, or drawing upon personal experiences and knowledge. By offering reliable and accurate information, we demonstrate our commitment to truthfulness and contribute to a more accurate understanding of faith-related topics. This helps correct misconceptions and encourages the other person to engage in a more informed and thoughtful discussion. Gently correcting misunderstandings is equally important. It is crucial to approach this with kindness, empathy, and respect. Rather than dismissing or belittling the other person's perspective, we can patiently and compassionately present alternative viewpoints or clarify misconceptions. This approach helps build trust and fosters a sense of openness and receptiveness to different ideas. When the person feels you are open to ideas, they feel more inclined to a conversation. This does not mean you are looking to change your beliefs. It means you are open to challenging your thinking so you may be better at sharing the gospel. By addressing misconceptions in a gentle manner, we create an environment where individuals feel heard and respected, enhancing the potential for a more constructive and fruitful conversation. How many times have you had pushy telemarketers call you and you were trying to be nice but they just kept pushing to the point you hung up on them. That's the type of evangelism we want to avoid.

As someone who has taught evangelism to people over the years, I would like to share some general advice before addressing common objections and how to handle them. Previously, I mentioned the gift of intellectual evangelism, where the goal is to appeal to someone's head and not their heart. In all other forms of evangelism, I advise appealing to people's hearts. When addressing common objections, aim to turn the conversation from a head conversation to a heart-to-heart interaction. Even if the discussion does not end in a person's salvation, there are still opportunities to plant seeds of Jesus through interactions. The results of our exchange are ultimately in God's hands. I have learned over the years that logic makes you think, and emotion makes you act. Using emotions and appealing to people's hearts and feelings is ok.

Remember Paul's writing in 1 Corinthians 3:6-9 (New International Version): "I planted the seed, Apollos watered it, but God has been making it grow. So neither the one who plants nor the one who waters is anything, but only God, who makes things grow. The one who plants and the one who waters have one purpose, and they will each be rewarded according to their own labor. For we are co-workers in God's service; you are God's field, God's building."

All in all, you and I are responsible for being witnesses to the world. The results are not up to us but to the individual God brought across our path. While it is exciting adding to the number of people that get saved through the efforts of evangelism, we cannot discount seed planting, nor can we discount the fact that the results are not up to us.

CHAPTER 6

Objection handling

The objections and answers outlined here are general themes, not exact wording. I recommend understanding the themes and how many answers can be the same, regardless of the points the other person is making. Here are some common objections to Christianity and how I have handled them in the past.

If God is loving, why does he send people to hell?

Let's think about the question why God would send people to hell despite His loving nature. It's essential to clarify a significant aspect of this issue. God, in His infinite love and mercy, does not actively send people to hell. Rather, He offers a way to avoid it through Jesus Christ. The choice to embrace Jesus and His salvation lies in our hands, for God has given us the gift of free will.

God's justice is intrinsic to His nature, and He grants us accountability for the decisions we make in life. It is up to us to choose whether we want to accept the love, forgiveness, and righteousness offered to us through Jesus or to walk our own path, being the masters of our own lives. In His love, God provided a solution to the predicament of sin and its consequences. He sent Jesus, His Son, to redeem humanity and bridge the gap between us and Him.

Through Jesus' sacrifice, we can receive God's grace and be reconciled with Him. However, this gift of salvation requires a response on our part. It demands that we make a choice – to accept Jesus as our Lord and Savior or to reject Him and His offer of forgiveness and lordship. God does not force anyone to follow Him, as that would negate the very essence of free will. In His wisdom, God honors our autonomy and allows us to decide our destiny. If we choose to remain distant from Him, rejecting His love and grace, then we are essentially choosing to bear the weight of our sins and their consequences.

Hell, in this context, is the consequence of our rejection of God's offer of salvation and the separation from Him that results from it. It's not that God sends people to hell, but rather, people make the choice to distance themselves from God and face the consequences of their decisions. In His love, God provides the means to avoid such a fate through Jesus Christ, but the ultimate choice rests with each individual. As we reflect on this matter, it becomes clear that God's love and justice are not in conflict. His love extends to every individual, offering the opportunity for redemption and reconciliation. In addition, His righteousness ensures that we are accountable for our choices and sins, allowing us to experience the consequences of our actions, whether for better or worse.

In conclusion, understanding why God "sends" people to hell is about recognizing the significance of free will in our relationship with Him. God, being just and loving, does not force anyone into a predetermined destiny. Instead, He offers the gift of salvation through Jesus and allows us to make our choices. Embracing Jesus leads to eternal life and a restored relationship with God, while rejecting Him results in the natural consequences of sin. God's love and justice intertwine harmoniously, giving us the freedom to choose our path while also being accountable for our decisions.

If God is so loving, why are there so many bad things in the world? (example: genocide, terrorism, cancer, sex trafficking, etc.)

The question of why there is so much suffering and evil in the world despite God's love is one that often leaves us doubtful of his existence and really confused. As a believer, I find comfort in knowing that God's love is not the cause of these terrible things but rather the source of hope and redemption in the face of darkness. God did not create us with sin; it entered the world when humans chose to disobey Him. He granted us the precious gift of free will, allowing us to make choices, but unfortunately, some of those choices have led to the spreading of evil and suffering.

In the face of this brokenness, God responded with boundless love and compassion. He sent His Son, Jesus Christ, to offer us a path of reconciliation. Through Jesus, we have the opportunity to believe in Him and restore our relationship with God. Jesus' teachings can profoundly impact how we live, enabling us to break free from the chains of sin and walk in righteousness.

Sin's essence has always been destructive, seeking to steal, kill, and destroy, as Jesus affirmed in John 10:10 (NIV): "The thief comes only to steal and kill and destroy; I have come that they may have life, and have it to the full." The consequences of sin often lead to suffering and pain, affecting individuals and societies alike. This means that all of sin profoundly impacts why the world is the way it is. Not that someone sinned and deserved sickness. Unfortunately, sickness, diseases, and death are a part of the fallen nature of a world full of sin. The sin came through the free will of rejecting God. The good news is that through free will, we can turn to God through Jesus Christ. While that is the best thing we can do here on earth, becoming a Christian does not mean all your problems go away. It means Jesus is with you through them. Because death will take us all, we have the assurance that death itself will no longer separate us from the Father but is the doorway to eternally being whole with him.

Even though the world is full of sin, evil, corruption, death, and disease, God's love shines through, even in the midst of our broken world. He does not force us into following a predestined path; instead, He grants us the gift of free will, allowing us to experience the natural consequences of our choices. It is an expression of His love that we have the freedom to choose. When we choose him and the path of righteousness, we choose the one who overcame evil, sickness, disease, and death. According to NIV John 16:33, "I have told you these things, so that in me you may have peace. In this world, you will have trouble. But take heart! I have overcome the world." **Human awareness of suffering, along with the consequences of evil and sin in the world, is crucial, as it prompts the recognition of the necessity for salvation. Without this awareness, the need for redemption would not be apparent. God's love remains an anchor of hope in a world of evil.**

God offers us healing, deliverance, and the strength to endure hardships. God does not stand idly by as we face suffering; He walks with us through the darkest valleys, offering comfort, peace, and strength. While we may not fully comprehend why bad things happen, we can find peace in God's love and His desire for our ultimate good. Through Jesus, we are invited to find hope, healing, and reconciliation. God's love empowers us to be a force for good, bringing light into the world's darkest corners and extending love and compassion to those who suffer.

In conclusion, evil and suffering in the world result from sin and the choices humanity has made. However, God's love remains steadfast, providing a way for his creation to find hope and healing through Jesus Christ. It is through God's love and the gift of free will that we can choose a path that leads to life and righteousness, even amidst the world's brokenness. As we embrace God's love and allow it to transform us, we become vessels of hope and change agents in a hurting world. "

If God can do anything, why can't He (insert task here)?"

When faced with challenging questions like, "If God can do anything, why can't He (insert task here)?" It's important to approach them with empathy and understanding. Such inquiries often arise from a place of deep contemplation, unresolved questions and a place of hurt. Acknowledging their significance is a vital first step. "Wow, that's truly a great and complex question," we might say, recognizing the depth of thought and emotion that underlies it. Understanding that these questions often stem from personal experiences and inner struggles, it's our responsibility to create a space for meaningful dialogue that can lead people toward God while addressing their concerns.

To answer this question, it's essential to begin by emphasizing the challenge of comprehending divine actions and intentions. Many of us have encountered situations where it seemed God should have intervened, yet He appeared silent. In those moments, we tend to place expectations on God, projecting how we believe He should act in a specific context. When these expectations remain unmet, it can lead to feelings of hurt, disappointment and broken trust. We put expectations on how God should act because we think it should be a certain way. This relationship is never any good. Whenever I put my expectations on others' behavior or how I want something, I set myself up for disappointment. This leads to unknowingly trying to control a person for a specific outcome. We must firmly hold to the truth that God's power is not restricted; rather, it is intricately intertwined with His character. He is consistently present with us, walking beside us in our most trying times. This unwavering presence demonstrates His love and faithfulness.

Additionally, it's important to recognize that God operates on a much larger canvas than our limited view of the here and now. He possesses an eternal plan of redemption that existed long before the dawn of the universe. This divine plan includes respecting humanity's free will, allowing us to experience both the consequences of our choices and the actions of others that impact our lives.

God's intervention is not confined to this specific moment in time and space. His actions and plans are rooted in His character, characterized by love, wisdom, and justice. In times of sickness and suffering, God provides healing in various ways. Physical healing can undoubtedly occur, but death is not the end for those who embrace salvation; it serves as a gateway to eternal wholeness in His presence.

In the face of pain, suffering, and evil, it's imperative to understand that this does not equate to God's absence or lack of power. We are constrained by our perception of time and space. At the same time, God exists beyond these boundaries, comprehending the end from the beginning. His goodness and power remain steadfast, even when we face adversity.

The sacrifice of Jesus epitomizes God's response to the world's pain and suffering. Jesus willingly endured pain and suffering, ultimately leading to redemption and reconciliation. This profound act ensures we need not confront the eternal anguish of separation from God's presence. In conclusion, it's essential to offer empathy and understanding when addressing challenging questions about God's actions and intentions or inactions. These questions are often rooted in personal experiences, and they should be acknowledged as such. Responding with love and wisdom, we can guide people toward a deeper understanding of God's character, His eternal plan, and His presence in their lives, even in the face of adversity.

In the Old Testament, we find examples of God extending grace and patience before resorting to judgment or destruction. The nation of Canaan, for instance, existed for approximately 430 years before God sent Israel to confront their rebellion. God sent Abraham to be a prophet of His grace and goodness to the people of Canaan. Another example is found in the story of Sodom and Gomorrah, where Abraham pleaded with God to spare the cities if there were even a few righteous people. Unfortunately, not enough righteous individuals were found, leading to the cities' destruction. In these instances, we witness God's mercy and willingness to extend grace, giving people ample opportunity to turn away from sin and towards Him. Even in this, God showed mercy to Abraham's family and to his nephew Lot by leading his family out of the city for safety even when there were not 10 righteous people in the city.

Even during the time of Noah, God provided a chance for repentance. Noah was called to build the Ark and warn the people of the coming flood for 100 years. The people had an opportunity to respond to God's message through Noah, but they rejected it, leading to the world's cleansing. It is essential to understand that God's actions in the Old Testament were not motivated by cruelty. God is holy, and anything that falls short of His holiness cannot be in His presence. The instances of judgment were often a response to the idolatry and wickedness that had permeated societies, leading them further away from God's will.

We often read the Old Testament in light of the knowledge of the New Testament. Before Jesus died on the cross, God handled people and sin differently. They were more accountable for their actions than we are. Is that Just? To God, it is. And if he truly is the creator of all things, then is it not right to handle situations the way he sees fit? We often attempt to comprehend and interpret God based on our limited perspectives and life experiences. However, we must recognize that if God is real, His knowledge and understanding far surpass ours, as He is the creator of all things. His ways are beyond our comprehension, and His wisdom is infinitely greater than anything we can fathom.

While it is natural for us to grapple with certain aspects of God's actions, particularly in the Old Testament, we must remember that our understanding is limited and imperfect. **God's love is not diminished by our struggles to comprehend His ways. His love is boundless and unwavering, transcending our human understanding.** While we might not always like or fully understand the reasons behind some of His actions in the Old Testament, it is vital to acknowledge His sovereignty and trust in His goodness.

It is essential to avoid the temptation of trying to impose our human judgments on God. He is not subject to our opinions or preferences. Instead, we are called to humbly submit to His authority and trust in His perfect wisdom. While there may be instances in the Old Testament that challenge our understanding, we must remember that God's ways are beyond our comprehension. Our faith lies in accepting that He is all-knowing and that His purposes are ultimately for the greater good, even if we cannot fully comprehend them.

In conclusion, while grappling with the events of the Old Testament can be difficult, we must approach these questions with humility and seek to understand God's character and motives. God's love is unchanging, and His ultimate plan for redemption was fulfilled through Jesus Christ. His actions in the Old Testament demonstrate His willingness to extend grace and patience, but also His commitment to justice and holiness. In seeking to understand these complexities, we can grow in our faith and trust in God's wisdom and love. When grappling with the complexities of understanding God, we must humbly acknowledge our limitations as finite beings.

Why does God send someone to hell who has never heard of Jesus:

When contemplating the question of why God would send someone to hell who has never heard of Jesus, there are various perspectives within Christian theology. One belief is that individuals who have never been exposed to the teachings of Jesus or the Bible but possess an inherent sense of right and wrong will be judged according to their actions. This belief says there is a higher power based on what knowledge they do have. It is essential to understand God does not actively send people to hell. Rather, it is sin that separates us from God and leads to our spiritual separation. God's desire is for all to come to repentance and salvation, as stated in 2 Peter 3:9. However, humans' free will and choices play a significant role in this process.

In NIV Romans 2:12-16 "**12** All who sin apart from the law will also perish apart from the law, and all who sin under the law will be judged by the law. **13** For it is not those who hear the law who are righteous in God's sight, but it is those who obey the law who will be declared righteous. **14** (Indeed, when Gentiles, who do not have the law, do by nature things required by the law, they are a law for themselves, even though they do not have the law.**15** They show that the requirements of the law are written on their hearts, their consciences also bearing witness, and their thoughts sometimes accusing them and at other times even defending them.) **16** This will take place on the day when God judges people's secrets through Jesus Christ, as my gospel declares."

This scripture highlights that regardless of their knowledge of the law or Jesus, people will be judged based on their actions and the moral law written on their hearts. This implies that everyone has a conscience and an innate understanding of right and wrong, influencing their behavior.

On the day of judgment, God will examine the secrets of people's hearts through Jesus Christ. This emphasizes the importance of personal accountability before God, regardless of whether individuals had access to specific religious teachings or not. Acknowledging that God's justice and mercy are beyond our complete comprehension is crucial. He is fair and righteous, and His judgments are based on His perfect knowledge and understanding.

In summary, how God judges those who have never heard of Jesus involves complex theological considerations. The belief that individuals will be judged according to the moral law written on their hearts highlights the role of personal responsibility and conscience. Ultimately, God's judgments are just and merciful, and we must trust in His wisdom and love, recognizing that He alone knows the hearts of all people.

I could never believe in a God who oppresses women.

The concern about God oppressing women seems to be a hot topic in today's culture. Because it is such a hot topic this makes it valid to address. When it comes to the reference to women wearing veils in 1 Corinthians 11:10, it is often misconstrued and requires a deeper understanding of the historical context and the Bible's overall perspective on women. Contrary to some misconceptions, the Bible and Christianity are among the first religious texts and beliefs which demonstrate respect for women. In the particular passage of 1 Corinthians 11, the Apostle Paul wrote to address cultural practices and offers women dignity and protection. During the time of the Roman Empire, it was customary for unmarried women to remain unveiled, which made them vulnerable to objectification and mistreatment by men. Paul's instruction to wear veils was not meant to oppress and hide women; instead, it symbolized commitment and protection within the context of marriage. In that society, the veil was akin to a modern wedding ring, signifying that a woman was married and under the care and guardianship of her husband. This practice aimed to safeguard women's dignity, purity, and honor within the cultural norms of the time. Moreover, it is crucial to recognize that women played vital roles in the life of Jesus and the early church.

Many women were among Jesus' followers, and they actively participated in spreading the gospel message. This was highly unusual and contrary to the cultural norms of that era, which often relegated women to subordinate roles. Throughout the New Testament, we see examples of women who played significant roles in the early church and the ministry of Jesus, including teachers, apostles, and prophets. Here are a few notable women: **Priscilla** and her husband Aquila were early Christian missionaries who worked closely with the apostle Paul. She is mentioned as a teacher of Apollos in Acts 18:26, demonstrating her role as an instructor in the faith. **Junia** is mentioned in Romans 16:7 as "outstanding among the apostles." This verse suggests that she held a prominent role in the early Christian community, possibly as an apostle. **Phoebe** mentioned in Romans 16:1-2, is referred to as a deacon and a benefactor of many, including the apostle Paul. Her role in the early church was undoubtedly significant. **Tabitha (or Dorcas) is** mentioned in Acts 9:36-42. She was a charitable woman known for her acts of kindness and was raised from the dead by the apostle Peter. Her story highlights the impact women had in early Christian communities. **Anna** is mentioned in Luke 2:36-38 as a prophetess who recognized Jesus as the Messiah when He was presented in the temple. Her testimony added to the early understanding of Jesus' significance. **Lydia**, a dealer in purple cloth, is mentioned in Acts 16:14-15. She is known for her hospitality and opened her home to Paul and his companions, supporting their ministry. **Euodia and Syntyche** These two women are mentioned in Philippians 4:2-3. Though their specific roles are not detailed, their names appear alongside other co-workers of Paul, indicating their involvement in the early Christian community.

It is essential to separate cultural practices from biblical principles. While some past cultural practices might appear restrictive to modern sensibilities, the Bible's overarching message upholds the dignity and worth of every individual, regardless of gender. Let's look at Jesus' Interactions with Women: In the Gospels, we find Jesus treating women with dignity, respect, and compassion. He engaged in meaningful conversations with women, even those who were considered outcasts or had questionable reputations. For instance, Jesus spoke with the Samaritan woman at the well (John 4), offering her living water and acknowledging her spiritual thirst. He defended the woman caught in adultery, showing mercy, and encouraging her to sin no more (John 8). Women as Witnesses to Jesus' Resurrection: In a significant cultural shift, women were the first witnesses to Jesus' resurrection according to all four Gospels (Matthew 28, Mark 16, Luke 24, John 20). In a time when women's testimony was often considered insignificant in legal matters, it is remarkable that the Gospel writers highlighted **Mary Magdalene**, a woman, as the primary witness to the resurrection of Jesus Christ. Thus making her the first true apostle. The apostle has encountered the risen Lord and proclaimed Him. The woman with the issue of blood is not only a healing miracle, but his interaction with her brought her dignity because she was unclean according to the law.

Emphasis on Equality: The Apostle Paul, in his letters, emphasizes the equality of men and women in Christ. Galatians 3:28 states, "There is neither Jew nor Gentile, neither slave nor free, nor is there male and female, for you are all one in Christ Jesus." This verse emphasizes that all believers, regardless of gender, have equal standing before God. Valuing all cultural standings including women, motherhood and Family: Christianity strongly emphasizes the sanctity of family and the role of mothers. The Bible celebrates motherhood and honors them. Several notable mothers are highlighted in the Bible for their significant roles and actions. Here are a few:

1. Eve: As the mother of humanity, Eve holds a foundational role in biblical narratives. Though often associated with the fall of mankind, she is also regarded as the mother of all living beings.
2. Sarah: Sarah is considered the matriarch of the Israelites, wife of Abraham, and mother of Isaac. Despite her old age, she miraculously gave birth to Isaac, fulfilling God's promise of descendants as numerous as the stars.
3. Rebecca: Rebecca, wife of Isaac and mother of Esau and Jacob, plays a crucial role in ensuring the fulfillment of God's promise of inheritance to Jacob, despite his brother Esau being the elder.
4. Rachel: Rachel, wife of Jacob, endured years of infertility before finally giving birth to Joseph and

Benjamin. Her love story with Jacob is one of the most famous in the Bible.
5. Hannah: Hannah's story is recounted in the books of Samuel. She fervently prayed for a child and was eventually blessed with Samuel, whom she dedicated to God's service.
6. Elisabeth (Elizabeth): The mother of John the Baptist, Elisabeth was barren until she miraculously conceived in her old age. Her story parallels that of Sarah and Hannah.
7. Mary: the mother of Jesus, is one of the most revered figures in Christianity. Her obedience to God's will and her role in giving birth to Jesus, the Son of God, make her central to the Christian faith.

These women each play significant roles in biblical narratives, demonstrating qualities of faith, perseverance, and devotion to God.

This next part is my personal belief; you, the reader, could study this more carefully. You can google search female-led Artemis cult in Ephesus. These women were leading many people astray with their false teachings. Because this was a big issue in their specific area and time, I believe Paul was talking to Timothy in the church of Ephesus not to let women speak because, in that area, women were not trusted due to this current cult situation. This, I believe, was done so that there would not be division in the church. That people could mentally separate the Church from the divisive cult in that city. I believe this letter of instruction was meant for that location. Not as the church as a whole.

In conclusion, the Bible and Christianity are early advocates of respecting women, recognizing their value, and challenging societal norms of their time. Understanding the historical context and the Bible's broader perspective helps us recognize the empowerment and dignity of women within Christianity. Christianity has a rich history of respecting and elevating the worth and dignity of women. From Jesus' interactions with women to their active roles in leadership and ministry, Christianity affirms the value of both men and women in the eyes of God. The contributions of women throughout Christian history continue to inspire and enrich the faith community.

I could never serve a God who does not love homosexuals.

I firmly believe that God's love knows no boundaries, and salvation is offered to all who repent of their sin, and this extends to every person He created, regardless of their sin or sexual orientation. Some may argue that God created certain individuals with homosexual tendencies. I believe that God did not create man with sin. God created man perfect. It was disobedience that brought sin into all of our lives. When I consider epigenetics from a biblical viewpoint, I see parallels with the concept of sin and its consequences being passed down through generations. In the Bible, we learn about the idea of generational sin, where the actions and choices of our ancestors can have lasting effects on subsequent generations. Just as epigenetic marks can influence the expression of certain genes, sin can leave a mark on our lives, affecting our behaviors and tendencies generationally as a spiritual and physically learned behavior. However, the beautiful message of Christianity is that through Jesus Christ, we are offered a new beginning and the opportunity to break free from the chains of sin. The Bible tells us that when we accept Jesus as our Savior, we become new creations in Him. In 2 Corinthians 5:17, it says, "Therefore, if anyone is in Christ, the new creation has come: The old has gone, the new is here!" (NIV).

This transformation in Christ is not just a spiritual concept; it can also have real-life implications in how our genes are expressed through epigenetic mechanisms. While our past and our ancestors' actions may have left marks on our DNA, the redemptive power of Jesus can break those chains, allowing us to live free from the burdens of sin. Just as epigenetic changes can be reversed through positive influences, our lives can be transformed when we surrender to Christ and embrace His love and forgiveness.

Epigenetics serves as a profound reminder of the complex interplay between our behaviors, environment, and biology. Epigenetics is a field of biology that explores how gene expression can be influenced and modified by factors other than changes in the underlying DNA sequence itself. The prefix "epi-" means "above" or "beyond," so epigenetics refers to changes that occur "above" or "on top of" the genetic code. These changes can affect how genes are activated or silenced without altering the DNA sequence. Epigenetic changes can be influenced by various factors, including environmental exposures, lifestyle choices, developmental stages, and even psychological experiences. Importantly, epigenetic modifications can be reversible and can also be passed down to future generations, potentially affecting the health and traits of offspring. From a biblical perspective, it aligns with the idea of generational sin, where the consequences of past actions can impact subsequent generations. However, the message of Christianity offers hope and redemption through Jesus Christ. By accepting Him, we become new creations, liberated from the chains of sin and set on a path of transformation and renewal. Epigenetics, with its reversible changes, mirrors this transformative power of Christ in our lives, reminding us of the grace and freedom found in Him.

While interpretations of scripture may vary, I hold onto the belief that God's love is not conditional and embraces everyone and offers salvation and redemption regardless of where their starting point is at. As Christians, we are called to follow Jesus, who taught us to love one another. Emphasizing love, compassion, grace, repentance and the transformational work of the cross should be at the core of our interactions with others, regardless of their sexual orientation.

In conclusion, my faith rests on the belief in a God whose love knows no bounds and extends to all, including homosexuals. I strive to approach this topic with understanding and empathy, recognizing the complexities and diversity of human experiences. While acknowledging the struggles some may face, I remain steadfast in the understanding that God's love is unconditional and the kindness of God that leads to repentance with the transformational work of the cross. This does not mean that we accept sin as ok and tell people to keep living a life of sin. We need to be clear in our stance. With that, we also need to take these same standards for all sins, not just one particular sin. My view on sin comes down to whether we recognize our actions as sinful or not. Regardless if it is homosexuality, or heterosexual sexuality or any other sin. Do we see it as sin and in need of personal transformation into Christ likeness or do we see it not as sin and no need for Christ's redemption of it. This is the difference of making Jesus Lord of one's life or an individual believing their ways are higher or better. Ironically, this is called PRIDE.

The concept of "I can't come to Jesus because I did XYZ sin."

When someone says, "I can't come to Jesus because I feel like I have committed a horrible sin," I am reminded of a simple analogy I often share with people. I ask them, "Do you have to get clean before you take a shower?" The answer, of course, is no. The whole purpose of a shower is to cleanse and refresh ourselves. Similarly, coming to Jesus and surrendering our lives to Him is like stepping into that shower of grace and forgiveness. We don't have to try to clean ourselves up first because it is Jesus who washes away our sins and makes us new.

Jesus' love and mercy are not dependent on our perfection or our past mistakes. He calls us to come to Him just as we are, with all our imperfections and brokenness. It is precisely in our brokenness that His love and light shines brightest. By accepting Jesus, we open ourselves to a transformative relationship with Him. As we walk with Him, our lives, hearts, and minds begin to be changed by His unconditional love and grace.

Remember, none of us are without sin; we all fall short in some way. That's why Jesus came – to offer His life as a sacrifice for our sins. It's not about our worthiness; it's about His grace and desire to bring healing and restoration to our lives. So, if you feel burdened by your past or present sins, know that Jesus is inviting you to lay those burdens at His feet. He longs to give you a new start and a renewed purpose. Come to Him just as you are, and let His love wash over you, cleansing and transforming you from the inside out. This is a process of transformation. Embrace the truth that in Christ, there is no sin too great, no heart too broken that His love cannot heal and redeem. Take that step of faith, and you will find that His grace is more than sufficient for you.

I could never serve a God that promotes slavery

The misguided thought comes from the NIV Ephesians 6:5-6: "Slaves, obey your earthly masters with respect and fear, and with sincerity of heart, just as you would obey Christ. Obey them not only to win their favor when their eye is on you, but like slaves of Christ, doing the will of God from your heart." It is very important to understand the cultural context that this is in and the overall arch of example the bible sets regarding this subject. Regarding culture, slavery was a prevalent practice in many different cultures and time periods. We see the types of slavery change from culture to culture. From hard labor to more personal assistance roles and all in between. As Paul is writing this he is doing so with the understanding that culturally slavery won't just stop, so the best example someone who is a slave can be is one who is serving Christ. Being a Godly example may help bring salvation and spiritual freedom to the house.

The Bible contains numerous instances that showcase God's heart for freedom and liberation from slavery, dispelling any notion that God endorses or approves of slavery. Here are a few key examples: **Exodus from Egypt** the story of the Israelites' being liberated from slavery in Egypt is a central theme in the Bible. In the book of Exodus, we see God's compassion for the oppressed and His direct intervention to free the Israelites from bondage. The entire narrative underscores God's desire for freedom and liberation as He works through Moses to lead His people out of slavery.

Year of Jubilee in the Old Testament, particularly in the book of Leviticus, God establishes the Year of Jubilee (Leviticus 25). This practice, occurring every 50 years, involved the release of slaves, the return of ancestral property, and debt forgiveness. The Year of Jubilee illustrates God's commitment to preventing long-term enslavement and promoting economic justice. **Prophet Isaiah's Message**: The prophet Isaiah repeatedly conveys God's displeasure with oppression and slavery. In Isaiah 58, God calls for the liberation of the oppressed, the breaking of every yoke, and the release of those held in bondage. These passages reflect God's heart for justice and freedom. **Jesus' Mission** and ministry was centered on bringing freedom to the oppressed and freedom from sin. In Luke 4:18-19, He quotes from Isaiah 61, proclaiming that He has come "to set the oppressed free" and "to proclaim the year of the Lord's favor." His work, including healing and liberating people from various forms of suffering, emphasizes God's commitment to freedom.

Paul's Letter to Philemon: In the New Testament, Paul's letter to Philemon addresses the issue of a runaway slave named Onesimus. Paul encourages Philemon to receive Onesimus as a brother, emphasizing the idea that in Christ, social distinctions and slavery should be abolished.

Galatians 3:28: In the Epistle to the Galatians, Paul writes, "There is neither Jew nor Gentile, neither slave nor free, nor is there male and female, for you are all one in Christ Jesus." This verse reinforces the idea that all men are created equal and that freedom comes through faith in Christ, irrespective of social status.

Freedom in Christ: The concept of freedom in Christ is a recurring theme in the New Testament. Believers are encouraged to stand firm in the freedom they have received (Galatians 5:1) and not be burdened again by a yoke of slavery. This freedom pertains to spiritual liberation but also embodies the principles of justice and equality. These are all wonderful examples from the Bible that clearly demonstrate God's heart for freedom and liberation from slavery. They reveal His consistent message of compassion for the oppressed and His desire for justice and equality among all people. God's actions and teachings throughout the Bible underscore the idea that He is not in favor of slavery but rather seeks the emancipation and dignity of all individuals.

"If God is so loving, why did He kill so many people in the Old Testament?"

Indeed, the question of God's actions in the Old Testament, particularly regarding the instances of destruction, is a deeply challenging one to grasp. As a believer, I find it essential to approach this question with humility and a willingness to seek understanding from God's perspective.

Firstly, it's crucial to acknowledge that no one stands innocent before God. All of humanity is guilty of sin, and our actions separate us from a perfect and holy God. We cannot earn our way into heaven through our own efforts or good deeds. The heart of the matter lies in God's ultimate solution to our sin problem – Jesus Christ. God's love was so profound that He sent His Son, Jesus, to take our place of suffering.

CHAPTER 7

Skills for Evangelism

Many of the skills listed in this short chapter have already been talked about and are currently sprinkled throughout the book. While I won't go back in-depth about them, I want to make a list for learning purposes.

1. **Prayer and Discernment:**
2. **Empathy and Active Listening**:
3. **Effective Communication**:
4. **Cultural Sensitivity:**
5. **Humility and Respect**:
6. **Flexibility and Adaptability**: Mission work has taught me a great deal about this topic. Many times in ministry, things are not going to go as you want or planned. This can be frustrating, and then if given into that frustration, it can hinder any work that you are doing. By being flexible, not only do you stay in peace, but you stay focused on what is most important: honoring God in all things that you do. Evangelism often requires adapting to different situations

and personalities. Being flexible and open-minded allows for meaningful connections and the ability to meet people where they are in their faith journey, even if you are in a frustrating circumstance.

7. **Integrity and Authenticity**:
8. **Humor and Joy**:
9. **Learn from Others**:
10. **Asking Provoking Questions**:
11. **Grow in Confidence:**
12. **Planning and preparing:**

CHAPTER 8

Stories of Lifestyle Evangelism

I have numerous personal stories about moments when God opened the doors for lifestyle evangelism to occur. The common thread in all these experiences is that they required me to step out of my comfort zone and be bold. It can be challenging to share your faith with others without boldness. After witnessing the meekness of my mother-in-law sharing the gospel with strangers, I believe anyone can summon the spirit of courage when the time arises. I want to share a few of my personal stories that have helped me understand the concept of lifestyle evangelism.

My wife and I were newlyweds living in an apartment complex on the top floor. One day, while driving home, I spotted a young Asian Indian lady, our neighbor, walking home about a mile and a half away from the apartment. I had not met her before but slowed down and offered her a ride home. This ended up being the icebreaker for my wife and me to get to know Shmeta. She came from India to get her pilot's license in Tulsa, Oklahoma. My wife and I begin inviting her over for dinner, and we got to know her better. On weekends, she liked to party, an area where we, as young people, couldn't relate to her. After a few visits, I asked her about her religion, and she didn't know what to believe. I wondered if she knew who Jesus was, and her answer astounded me. She said, "Yes, that's the man who followed me for three days." I asked her what she meant. She told us that before coming to America, a spiritual being named Jesus visited her and followed her around for three days, talking to her and telling her about himself. She said she wanted to know more about him and what it means to be a Christian. We invited her to church with us the next day, and she accepted. At the end of the service, the church was doing communion, which we did by intinction. This is where you go to one of the elders, receive the bread, and dip it into the juice. Shmeta wanted to take communion with us. Before going up, I explained to her that Christians do this after accepting Jesus as Lord and Savior. I explained what the juice and the bread were. I told her that before she went up, she would need to believe this and accept Jesus as her Lord and Savior. And she did just that.

All of this came into being because I gave her a ride, an act of service. Then it led to a neighborly relationship, which led to more acts of service by having her over for dinner, followed by invitational evangelism to church, where she heard the teachings and accepted Jesus. There are many different styles of evangelism that took place during this relationship and they were all natural to the part of the relationship that we were in.

Evangelism is not some big to-do event. It is simply living life with others. Back in 2009, I had the opportunity to take a solo mission trip to the Philippines. It was a challenging experience as I developed food poisoning within a few days of arrival. This was around the same time H1N1 was a concern, and when I went to the hospital, I was quarantined for seven days. This was a challenging moment in my life, with limited visitors and no TV. I felt like I was in prison and lost 40 pounds in two weeks from being unable to eat and being attached to a drip IV. It was mentally challenging thinking I was dying in a third-world hospital.

Considering the circumstances, I was awarded a $1,000 scholarship from the BJ Memorial Scholarships for Missions, which was a special recognition for me. BJ was a young man who became sick on a mission trip overseas and died after returning to the US. This happened a few days before I left for my trip. Receiving this scholarship and being in the hospital for a sickness that was not diagnosed at the time left me with a crippling fear.

God asked me if I wanted to give up and go home or if I wanted to stick it out for the next two months. Because the funding for this trip was miraculous and all came in the last week before my trip, I felt God was opening the doors for me to go. I had been raising funds for a whole year prior to that. I told God that I wanted to stick it out, and the pastor I was staying with helped me recover by taking me out of the hospital, as I was not receiving proper care there. Over the next few months, I focused on recovering from my illness.

I could not do as much ministry work as I had originally planned. Still, I did have the opportunity to take a trip to another island. It was an overnight boat ride to get there, and once we landed, we took a narrow riverboat for four hours to reach a remote area. The huts were built on long sticks or tied down on floating logs and were located in a major flood area that would be flooded for half the year.

During my visit, I was able to build relationships with some of the young and middle-aged men in the village by playing basketball on a concrete court. I was one of the tallest people there, standing at 5'10", which gave me an advantage, even with my lack of basketball skills. One of the men, named Robert, and I formed a special bond, even though we couldn't communicate well. We had a high level of chemistry playing basketball together, and we won every game that we were on the same team. At some point, other players wanted us on different teams.

On the last night in the village, I had a special moment with Robert. I wrote about it in my journal titled "Candlelight Love." here is that entry. I was asked if doing missions was a way for me to remember Jesus Christ and if it helped me see God more clearly and grow my relationship with Him. Although I was never able to answer the man who lived in the village, I thought about what he said. I realized that the people in the village were trying to bless me and were hurt when they couldn't. They didn't have much, with no access to fresh water or bathrooms, but they still tried to make me comfortable. I had to change my thinking from giving to receiving, as giving would send the message that what they had was not good enough.

Receiving from them meant more than anything I could have given them. To live like them and to be with them and share what they had, I became a part of or one with them. At the end of my trip, they were so thankful for me coming and being a part of their families. I was told so many times that they were blessed because I wanted to live like them. By being with them, it showed that I saw value in what they had, and that I accepted them as a human that God loved. So, my actions in being in a relationship with them opened the doors for me to love them and to minister to them the way Jesus ministered to Zacchaeus.

There was a moment last night when I was sleeping on the hardwood floor when my new friend and basketball partner, Robert, came over to me with a candle and held it up to my face and, in his broken English, said, "You sleep?" I rolled over and looked at him with a smile, and said, "No." He said, "Okay." He sat down right by me. God, in that moment, started to do something in my heart. I sat up and asked him if he wanted to talk. He said, "Okay." He put his hand over his heart and, extended it to me, and said, "I love you. (brotherly love) Will you remember me?" I told him that I would always remember him. At that time, I walked to my bag, praying that there would be something in there that I could give him. Right before I left, I decided to take a necklace that my sister-in-law gave me for my birthday several years ago. I saw it, took it out, and without hesitation, I gave it to him.

Back in the United States, so many people have asked for this necklace over the years, but it had a lot of meaning and value to me because a family member gave it to me.

However, at that moment, I knew this was the right place to give it as a gift. He asked me if we could be friends, and I said, "Yes, but we can even be brothers." He already was a believer, but being brothers means more than friends. His face when I gave him the necklace, became overwhelmed, and tears filled his eyes. He began to say, "You give me in remembrance of you?" I said, "Yes, I will leave a little bit of me with you so that you'll always remember me." He said, "I can't repay you for this gift. I have nothing that I could give you because I am so poor." I told him that I did not give to get something from him but gave this to him because I loved him as well. "Do this in remembrance of me," as Jesus broke the bread and passed it to his disciples and poured out the wine as an example of him pouring out his life for others. I believe that communion is a very important part of the Christian faith. Still, I find that it is much more important to live life like communion than just taking communion itself.

Putting our body or flesh in a place of sacrifice for others and pouring out our lives for the cause of others and Christ. To me, God showed me his gift of salvation and his love that I could never have paid for. I am so poor that I could never have had any worthiness to accept it. Candlelight Love is about seeing how much more I am like Robert than I think. But in this way, I am poor, and the one who is homeless, the one who can't afford anything that God has ever given me. But, out of love, I am able to receive a gift that means more than anything.

I say that to say this: maybe after realizing just how much God has given us, we might be able to look past the things we have and understand the value of what he has given, and just maybe then we'll be better givers after seeing and understanding what he's given us. This is the conclusion of my journal entry.

I had to leave the village and wasn't sure if I would ever see Robert again, but years later, I found out he stepped away from Christianity after losing a child to a brain tumor. I sent a message to Robert through my pastor friend, telling him to hold on to God and trust in Jesus even in his pain. To trust God in the process of hurt and to get back in the church. My pastor friend was going back to preach on the island where Robert lives. But Robert lives a fair way from the location my pastor friend would be. 4 hours by canoe boat up the river. To my surprise, Robert came down the river to see if I had sent him a message through my friend. He had no clue if I would have or not but in faith he went to go see my pastor friend hoping I had sent him greetings.

Robert attended the meeting that my pastor friend held and recommitted his life to the Lord after receiving my message. Over the years, Robert moved to a larger city, and we communicated occasionally through Facebook with a translator. This relationship and connection built by God is a reminder that even when time and distance seem like they would kill a relationship, God's seeds bear fruit years later. We must trust in the Lord and the process and have faith in the seeds we plant. God can restore people in your life to be a witness to them. Trust in God to build relationships with others even if it does not seem like you will make a difference in the amount of time you are in someone's life because you can and I believe you will.

One of the most impactful moments in my life in receiving God's love from another person happened between my sophomore and junior years of college. It all started on the last day of school, my freshman year. I was attending chapel service at Oral Roberts University, and during the service, I felt God asking me to be a chaplain next year on a dorm floor. After lunch, I went to the Chaplains office to see if I could still sign up. I knew the program had selected chaplains and floor placement for the following year. But I wanted to be obedient to the Lord. I arrived at the office, and the director asked who sent me. I told him no one. We continued to talk, and he again asked me who sent me. I told him again No one. After more conversation, he asked me again who sent me to his office, and I said God told me to come. Why do you ask? He told me he saw me in the chapel and did not know who I was but felt God had told him I was to be a chaplain. My GPA was not high enough to be a chaplain, and I told him I had learning disabilities. He was sympathetic and understood and told me they would accept me anyway.

The following year, I was placed on a challenging floor. The last Chaplin kept coming back and making it hard for me to do my job. I was a little stricter in actually having a floor service than the last guy was. The floor and I overall were not a great fit. So the floor made a petition full of lies to get me kicked off the floor and out of the program. This was before Christmas break sophomore year. I heard nothing of this letter before I left. Now that break was over I came back for school a few days early. I remember praying this prayer to the Lord. I asked him to make me more like him and change me at my own cost. That is a dangerous prayer. The next day, I got called into the director's office, and he told me that my grades were too bad for me to continue in the program and that he was disappointed with my schooling. He cut straight into a wound I have carried my whole life. Knowing I had learning disabilities. He used that against me to remove me. He told me I could still be in the program but would lose my scholarship and the floor. I found out later that he offered this to me to try to save face and that he did not want me and did not expect me to say yes. I did, however, say yes because I felt God called me to serve the program. A few weeks went by, and some guys on my old floor came to me and told me that they wanted me to know they had nothing to do with the letter full of lies that got me removed. I asked what letter. Then, they began to tell me all the horrible things that the floor accused me of. I was so hurt. Not by the floor but by the leadership.

That he would tell me my schooling got me kicked out of the program, not this letter. I never got a chance to defend myself. This was a deep wound.

Moving on into my junior year, there was a new chaplain director. A great man by the name of Eric Peterson. Though I did not know he was a great man at the time. All I knew was that he held the position of the guy that last hurt me. I was not in the program my junior year. But many times, walking past Eric, I was standoffish. He always singled me out and told me hello. Then, after a while, he would say I love you man, have a great day in passing. This angered me so much. One day, he approached me and asked to meet me in his office to hear about my experience with the program. I told him he did not want that and that I had nothing good to say. He told me that is why he wanted to meet me. So I went to his office and talked with him, telling him everything that had happened. At the end of my sharing the story, he got up from behind his desk, came over to me and looked me in the eye, and said Evan, I am so sorry. Will you forgive me? I said what do you mean? You had nothing to do with this. Someone else did. Why are you saying this? He told me, I hold the position of the person that wronged you, so therefor I wronged you. I am asking for your forgiveness. At that moment, I broke. I started crying, and he hugged me. I told him yes, I forgive you.

Eric became a conduit of grace and forgiveness in my life. He helped me to let go of my bitterness and anger by taking on someone else's sin and asking me to forgive him. This was such a fantastic picture of what Jesus did for us. This was such a lesson to me that day and has been a critical part of my style of evangelism. I meet people all the time hurt by other Christians, and because of what Eric did for me and the example he set, that taught me that I can also take on that role for other people to help them release bitterness and anger. This allows the person to see God's love and grace in their life and no longer have to carry the hurt. They get to see Jesus. Thank you, Eric. I am so grateful to you.

In the final part of this chapter the spotlight falls on a remarkable man named Ted Robertson, affectionately known as Robertson Tires and celebrated as the GODFATHER of marketplace ministry in Tulsa, Oklahoma. Ted's legacy in the realm of marketplace ministry is nothing short of legendary, leaving an indelible mark on the community he served.

Ted's impact is far-reaching; he has been a mentor to countless individuals and the driving force behind the formation of various Christian groups of businessmen, the most recent being Tulsa Christian Businessmen. This group operates with a clear mission: to foster a sense of community among Christian businessmen while extending invitations to non-believers in the business world to join their monthly lunches. These gatherings feature guest speakers sharing personal testimonies and insights into how God has worked in their businesses. The group also engages in monthly charitable fundraising, hosts small mentorship meetings, and occasionally conducts small group Bible studies.

At the age of 94, Ted continues to be a dynamic force within the group he founded, tirelessly working to nurture the next generation of leaders. His commitment to combining business and life with ministry has been a source of inspiration for many, with numerous men attributing the incredible transformations in their lives to Ted's influence.

For me personally, Ted's actions and the groups he helped create have been transformative. Initially aspiring to enter vocational ministry, my journey, intertwined with the Young Businessmen of Tulsa and Tulsa Christian Businessmen, revealed the profound integration of ministry into everyday life and the marketplace. These experiences debunked the notion of separate spheres for business and ministry, showing me that they could coexist harmoniously.

The impact of Ted's influence extends far beyond our immediate circle. Many individuals, shaped by Ted's guidance, have gone on to undertake similar initiatives, leaving an enduring impact on the community. Reflecting on Ted's life unveils a ripple effect – a powerful testament to the profound and inspirational outcomes that consistency, coupled with a heart to serve others for Christ, can yield. It's a lesson we can all glean from and aspire to embody in our own lives.

CHAPTER 9

Presence based evangelism

Presence-based evangelism is about being led by the Holy Spirit in ministering to others in your everyday life and, hearing God and recognizing his presence in life and in ministry through the holy spirit. In order to do presence-based ministry, you have to live a presence-based life. Ministry will happen out of the overflow of God's presence in your life. If not done this way, then you are emptying yourself, and you were never created to do that. It is easy to get caught up in trying to do ministry to get closer to God, but the ministry has to happen out of use being in God's presence and his leading. Just as we aim to live a presence-based life in our relationship with God, so do we in our approach to evangelism. In presence-based evangelism, our goal is to be led by the Holy Spirit in ministering to others and recognizing our dependence on God's presence in our own lives. We understand that true ministry must flow from the overflow of God's presence within us.

Recognizing God's presence in our lives is essential because it acknowledges the relational connection we have with our Creator. When we are aware of His presence, we become attuned to His guidance, comfort, and wisdom. It is through this recognition that we can truly experience a deeper and more meaningful relationship with Him. Not because we get something from him but because he is present in our lives. Just as recognizing God's presence is essential in our relationship with Him, it's also crucial in evangelism. When we evangelize, we do so with the awareness that God's presence is not only within us but desires to manifest in the lives of those we reach out to. This recognition strengthens our trust in His guidance and prepares us to be vessels through which His presence can touch others. Practicing the presence of God allows us to cultivate a constant awareness of His love and faithfulness. It reminds us that we are never alone, even in the most challenging times. This awareness empowers us to trust in His plans, seek His direction, and find comfort in His presence.

When we actively seek God's presence, we become more sensitive to His voice and leading. This sensitivity enables us to discern His will and align our lives with His purposes. As we surrender our hurts, fears, and issues, we experience a greater sense of fulfillment knowing that God is with us through the hurt and the pain, turning these things into purpose, and knowing that we are living out His design in our lives accordance with the way he made me.

Recognizing God's presence helps us to live in gratitude and thanksgiving. When we are aware of His constant presence and the blessings He bestows upon us, our hearts overflow with gratitude. This attitude of gratitude transforms our perspective, allowing us to see the world through the lens of His goodness and grace instead of our own issues and hurts.

The practice of recognizing God's presence in our lives instills a sense of awe and reverence. It reminds us of His majesty, sovereignty, and holiness. This awareness deepens our worship and adoration for Him, fostering a greater intimacy and awe-filled reverence in our relationship with Him. As we acknowledge God's presence in our lives, we become attuned to His guidance, wisdom, and comfort. Similarly, in evangelism, our aim is to establish an intimate connection with those we seek to reach. By sharing God's love and truth, we introduce others to the comforting and transformative presence of God.

We invite Him into every aspect of our lives by acknowledging God's presence. This empowers us to surrender our burdens, fears and struggles to Him. It opens the door for His healing, restoration, and transformation to take place, leading to a greater sense of peace, joy, and wholeness.

Recognizing God's presence fuels our faith. God's presence strengthens our trust in Him. When we understand that He is with us, we find confidence in His promises and assurance in His faithfulness. This deepened faith empowers us to step out in obedience, overcome obstacles, and walk boldly in the calling He has placed upon our lives.

The practice of recognizing God's presence helps us to develop a constant state of prayer and communication with Him. It prompts us to seek His guidance, intercede for others, and express our desires, struggles, and thanksgiving.

145

This ongoing dialogue fosters a deeper intimacy and connection with Him, allowing us to experience His love, and respond to His leading in a more profound way.

Recognizing God's presence in our lives reminds us of our identity as His beloved children. It affirms that we are not alone, insignificant, or forgotten but rather cherished and known by our heavenly Father. This recognition empowers us to live with confidence, knowing that we are deeply loved and valued by the One who created us. Just as recognizing God's presence deepens our relationship with Him, our evangelism efforts prioritize building relationships with those we are reaching out to. It's not just about sharing a message but forming genuine connections, allowing people to experience the love and presence of God through ultimately, recognizing and practicing God's presence in our lives empowers us as His creation to live a life that glorifies Him. It equips us to reflect His love, grace, and truth to the world around us. By recognizing His presence, we become vessels through which His kingdom can be manifested, making a positive impact on others, and bringing glory to His name.

While there are many ways to engage in practicing the presence of God, here are some of my own practices. Practice God's presence can happen through praise and worship. As the bible mentioned, God inhabits the praises of His people. Engaging in heartfelt worship through singing, praying, or expressing gratitude creates an atmosphere where we invite God's presence to manifest and dwell among us. By setting aside time for intentional praise, we cultivate a deeper connection with Him and open ourselves to His transforming power.

Another powerful way to practice God's presence is by immersing ourselves in His living Word. The Bible is more than just a collection of stories; it is a divine revelation of God's character, His will, and His promises for us. Regularly reading and studying Scripture allows us to encounter God's presence through His inspired words. It is in His Word that we find guidance, comfort, and encouragement in our daily lives.

Daily discipline plays a significant role in practicing God's presence. For the longest time, I have felt like it was a religious obligation that I had to do, but I learned that if something is important to me, it needs to be on my calendar. Though I still struggle to prioritize what is most important, we intentionally create space for God and the manifestation of his presence in our lives. This can involve daily dedicated time for stillness and resting in him. I always encourage people to live in a community as a way to see and feel God's presence. Meditation on one scripter. Such disciplines help us to tune our hearts and minds to God's presence, allowing us to experience His peace, guidance, and transformative power in our lives. I can honestly say I often struggle with creating these designated spaces and time to do that. Does that mean I am less loved or experience God's presence less? I believe what we focus on expands in our lives. So, I tend to focus on God and his presence in my life throughout the whole day, not just at a specific time. In essence, I am living with God in all things that I am doing. Through this process, we get to see the effects of how God intends this relationship to be.

Cultivating a lifestyle of prayer is practicing God's presence. Prayer is not just a religious ritual but a vital means of communication with our Creator. By engaging in regular, heartfelt conversations with God, we invite His presence into our lives. It is through prayer that we pour out our hearts, seek His guidance, intercede for others, and experience the intimacy of a relationship with Him. Prayer is also more than us communicating to God. Prayer is also silent listening. If prayer is a conversation with God, then listening is also a part of prayer because you cannot have a conversation without both parties talking and listening.

Another way to practice God's presence is through acts of service and love towards others. When we extend kindness, compassion, and forgiveness to those around us, we embody God's presence in the world. By intentionally reflecting His character in our actions, we become vessels through which His love and grace can flow to others, making a tangible impact and pointing them to His goodness. Practicing gratitude is a transformative way to cultivate God's presence in our lives. When we intentionally acknowledge and give thanks for His blessings, big and small, we shift our focus from our circumstances to His faithfulness. Gratitude opens our hearts to recognize His presence in every aspect of our lives and cultivates a spirit of contentment and joy.

I hear people say all the time that I don't need to go to church to be a Christian. While true, we miss such an important part of what God has for us. Engaging in regular fellowship and community with other believers is vital for practicing God's presence. When we gather with like-minded individuals, we create an environment where God's presence can be tangibly felt. Through worshiping, praying, and studying God's Word together, we encourage and sharpen one another in our faith, deepening our connection with God and each other. Practicing solitude is another powerful way to experience God's presence. In the midst of our busy lives, taking intentional moments to be still and quiet allows us to listen and be attentive to His voice. It is in the silence that we can discern His leading, receive His comfort, and experience His peace that surpasses all understanding. This type of silence is different from prayer silence. This is a type of short-term fasting.

Engaging in acts of self-reflection and examination helps us practice God's presence. Taking time to evaluate our thoughts, attitudes, and actions in light of His truth allows us to invite His transformative presence into areas that need growth and healing. Through introspection and repentance, we position ourselves to experience His forgiveness and restoration.

Finally, maintaining an attitude of surrender and obedience is crucial for practicing God's presence. By surrendering our will and desires to Him and choosing to walk in obedience to His commands, we open ourselves to a deeper experience of His presence and power. Obedience allows us to align our lives with His purposes, enabling His presence to flow through us and impact the world around us. As human beings, we are uniquely fashioned as image-bearers of God. This means that we are created in a way that reflects the character and nature of our Creator. Just as an image reflects the likeness of the one it represents; we bear the imprint of God's divine attributes within us.

One of the primary reasons for our existence is to cultivate a deep and meaningful relationship with God. We have been designed with the capacity to know Him intimately, to communicate with Him, and to experience His love and presence in our lives. This relational aspect of our being sets us apart from the rest of creation and brings us into a state of communion with our heavenly Father.

Furthermore, our purpose as image-bearers extends beyond our personal relationship with God. We are called to reflect His glory to the world around us. Just as a mirror reflects the image before it, we are meant to showcase God's goodness, love, and righteousness in our words, actions, and attitudes. By living in accordance with His will and displaying His character, we become ambassadors of His kingdom on Earth.

Our role as image bearers also involves actively participating in the advancement of God's kingdom. This means seeking to bring His love and mercy into every sphere of our influence – be it our families, workplaces, communities, or the world at large. Through our actions and efforts, we can contribute to the transformation of society and the spreading of God's reign, bringing His light to dark places and embodying His values in all that we do.

Ultimately, our journey as image bearers finds its fulfillment when we finally see God face to face. This speaks of the day when we will be in His presence fully, experiencing His glory without any hindrance. It is a future hope that fuels our present walk, knowing that one day we will intimately know and be known by the One who created us. Until that day comes, we press on, seeking to fulfill our purpose as image bearers, living in relationship with God, reflecting His glory, and advancing His kingdom.

CHAPTER 10

Leading with prayer?

L eading with prayer is such a powerful approach to ministry, and it's something that resonates deeply with me. You see, I've always believed that prayer is the foundation of any meaningful interaction or outreach effort.

When I think about reaching out to others, especially those who may be going through tough times, my instinct is always to start with prayer. It's like laying a solid groundwork before building anything else. Prayer sets the tone, inviting God's presence and guidance into the situation.

Sometimes, diving straight into evangelism can feel overwhelming or even off-putting for people. But offering to pray for someone? That's something almost universally accepted, regardless of someone's beliefs or background. It's a simple yet profound gesture of care and compassion.

I've found that when I offer to pray for someone, especially when they seem like they're having a rough day or struggling with something, it often opens doors that might otherwise remain closed. It's like an invitation for them to share their burdens, knowing that someone genuinely cares and is willing to stand with them in prayer.

Now, I'll be honest, there have been times when I've felt uncertain about what to pray or how to pray in those moments. But you know what? That's okay. I've come to realize that it's not about saying the perfect words or having all the answers. It's about being present, being willing to listen, and allowing the Holy Spirit to work through me.

In those moments of prayer, I've seen God move in miraculous ways. I've witnessed hearts soften, burdens lifted, and lives transformed. And it's all because we dared to lead with prayer – to put our trust in God and His power to bring about healing and restoration.

So, as I write about leading with prayer in my chapter, I want to emphasize this foundational principle: **prayer is not just a precursor to ministry; it is ministry**. It's the heartbeat of everything we do, the thread that connects us to God and to one another. And when we lead with prayer, **we're not only opening doors for ministry; we're inviting God to work in and through us in ways we could never imagine**.

1. Knowing what to pray for: Sometimes, people will let you pray for them, but they won't tell you what they want prayer for. I often push a little to get specific but I start praying even if they give me nothing to pray for, or ask for through prayer. This is one of my favorite moments because it puts it all in God's hands on how we should pray. The responsibility on our part is to hear God's heart for the other person. I often find that in moments like this, I pray exactly what the person needs down to specific situations that are going on in their lives. I feel that God gives me ideas that come to mind when I am praying. The most common question I get after praying with people is how did you know all of that. I tell them I don't, but the lord does, and he is the one who told me how to pray for you because he loves you and wants you to know that he is with you.

Before approaching someone with the Gospel, we should ask the Holy Spirit to guide our interactions. We should ask Him to give us wisdom and discernment and to open the hearts of those we speak to so they may experience the love of God through us and we can plant seeds of relationship with Jesus in their lives or lead them in salvation.

2. Praying for opportunities: This is one way the Holy Spirit may lead us in Evangelism. I remember it was 2008, and I wanted to go on a mission trip through my college, Oral Roberts University. We had a team of eight going to the Czech Republic and Romania. I was looking forward to this trip. As the trip was coming closer, our eight-person team dropped down to a four-person team. If any of the four people left dropped out, the team would be dissolved, and students would be put on other trips. Shortly after that announcement was made, I felt like I heard the Holy Spirit tell me he wanted me to stay in Tulsa that summer because he had something significant he wanted me to do. I knew I heard God, so it was easy to make up my mind about not going on the trip, but I had to have some really hard conversations with my team, the team leader, and the mission's coordinator. They were all trying to talk me out of that decision.

Well, I stayed in Tulsa, and the trip got disbanded. Remember that snow cone job I was telling you about? I got a job working in a snow cone stand that summer. 6 days a week, ten to twelve hours a day. Through that time, God not only healed me of the learning disabilities that I had, but I became more aware of his presence through prayer and depended my relationship with Jesus. So much ministry started happening out of the snow cone shack. People were coming to me because God was leading them. I did not have to try to force the door of the ministry open. I prayed that God would open doors. All I had to do was recognize them. **God will always provide open doors of ministry, even if it seems like he is shutting others.**

The Holy Spirit may lead us to certain people or situations where we have the opportunity to share the Gospel, where otherwise we would not have had. If we did not listen, he might not bring people to us. We should be open and sensitive to these opportunities and trust that the Holy Spirit is guiding us to them and that we can recognize them when they occur.

3. Words of knowledge through prayer, and spiritual gifts: These are ways in which the Holy Spirit may lead us in Evangelism. The Holy Spirit may give us specific words through prophecy or an understanding through the gift of discernment or actions to share with others that will draw them to Christ. We should listen to these promptings and trust that the Holy Spirit is using us to reach others for Christ. Prophetic words to people are like water on a hot day. They bring refreshment and life to the soul when it is given from the direction of the Holy Spirit. God has gifted his children with specific gifts so we can share his goodness with others. These gifts will encourage us to grow in our relationship with Jesus through the Holy Spirit.

Areas of life people want prayed for.

Finances: There has always been uncertainty with people's finances. The majority of people live paycheck to paycheck. Philippians 4:19 NIV And my God will meet all your needs according to the riches of his glory in Christ Jesus. Deuteronomy 8:12 NIV 12 The LORD will open the heavens, the storehouse of his bounty, to send rain on your land in season and to bless all the work of your hands. You will lend to many nations but will borrow from none.

Work: I remember there was a time in my life when I could not land a job to save my life. I worked a lot of temp jobs, or I ended up working in a bad situation because I took the first job that was open. I had over 21 jobs in 4 years between 2010 and 2014. It was stressful. Not working can feel degrading. When praying with someone over this area, pray for the job and their identity. Psalm 90:17 NIV 17 May the favor of the Lord our God rest on us; establish the work of our hands for us, yes, establish the work of our hands. Ephesians 2:10 NIV 10 For we are God's handiwork, created in Christ Jesus to do good works, which God prepared in advance for us to do.

Broken Relationships: Many people have broken marriages and broken relationships with family members and other loved ones. This weighs heavily on a lot of people's hearts. Hebrews 10:24-25 NIV 24 And let us consider how we may spur one another on toward love and good deeds,

25 not giving up meeting together, as some are in the habit of doing, but encouraging one another – and all the more as you see the Day approaching. Ephesians 4:32 NIV 32 Be kind and compassionate to one another, forgiving each other, just as in Christ God forgave you.

Healing and Health: Isaiah 53:5 NIV 5 But he was pierced for our transgressions, he was crushed for our iniquities; the punishment that brought us peace was on him, and by his wounds we are healed. 2 Chronicles 7:14 NIV If the people who are called by my name humble themselves and pray and seek my face and turn from their wicked ways, then I will hear from heaven and will forgive their sin and heal their land.

Peace over anxiety and Depression: Currently, there are statistics floating around that 25% of the population in America struggles with anxiety. As of now, I am currently one of them. Many things go into people having this problem, such as food, overall health, environment, and perceived life as well as genetics. When I pray with people who also struggle with this, I give them advice I have used in my life. Feel free to do the same when you can speak from experience. I am giving you these scriptures so you know what the word of God says and so that you can stand on them. You can even offer them to the person you talking to. When it comes to anxiety and depression There is far more to it then just saying scripture. Make sure when you give scripture you not say read the bible more and you will be better. Pray more and you will be better. Let this person know that Jesus is with them in the midst of their anxiety and that they can stand on God's word and know that this is not a forever thing in their life. It's important to let the person know that anxiety is not a sign of weakness or lack of faith. Instead, it's a human experience that many people go through, and it's okay to seek help and support. Encouraging them to lean on their faith and trust in God's promises can provide strength and hope as they navigate their journey towards healing.

Ultimately, our goal should be to offer love, support, and practical resources to help them overcome their anxiety. By combining the comfort of scripture with understanding and empathy, we can walk alongside them on the path to wholeness and restoration.

Philippians 4:6-7 Do not be anxious about anything, but in every situation, by prayer and petition, with thanksgiving, present your requests to God. 7 And the peace of God, which transcends all understanding, will guard your hearts and your minds in Christ Jesus. Matthew 6:25-32 NIV 25 "Therefore I tell you, do not worry about your life, what you will eat or drink; or about your body, what you will wear. Isn't life more than food and the body more than clothes? 26 Look at the birds of the air; they do not sow or reap or store away in barns, and yet your heavenly Father feeds them. Are you not much more valuable than they?27 Can any one of you, by worrying, add a single hour to your life? 28 "And why do you worry about clothes? See how the flowers of the field grow. They do not labor or spin.29 Yet I tell you that not even Solomon in all his splendor was dressed like one of these.30 If that is how God clothes the grass of the field, which is here today and tomorrow is thrown into the fire, will he not much more clothe you-you of little faith? 31 So do not worry, saying, 'What shall we eat?' or 'What shall we drink?' or 'What shall we wear?' 32 For the pagans run after all these things, and your heavenly Father knows that you need them.

Grief: At some point in our lives, we will all go through the grief of losing a loved one. If you have had this happen, it is much easier to relate to someone going through grief. If you have not yet, you can imagine what that would be like to lose a loved one. Grief affects so many areas of a person's life. When dealing with grief, people often don't know what to say, so they say something dumb like well, now they are in heaven and not in pain anymore or the Lord called said person home. There are other folks who say nothing. Nothing is better than saying something dumb. The person in grief won't tell you what you said was dumb, most of the time, but it does add to the hurt. I have often found that comedy is a great icebreaker in situations like this.

But it has to be led by God and not just forced. You're not there to do damage control for someone's grief. When Jesus went to raise Lazarus from the dead, before he did, he cried with the family over his death, even knowing full well he was going to raise him. The best ministry is that of love. I love people. You don't have the right words. Follow the example of Jesus and be compassionate in these moments. I always encourage people in their grief that this time of their life is a great time to use that feeling of desperation and point it towards God because he will comfort you. A few days after losing our daughter I got a call from the funeral home saying they have yet to receive her body and if they don't have it they cannot do the funeral. We had 48 hours to go. I called the hospital and the nurse said they did not have it; the transport company took her for the autopsy. I called the autopsy location, and they said she was never received.

I called the transport company and they said the hospital never gave the body to them. Can you imagine how much hurt and pain all this was causing me? I am trying to grieve, and this is going on. I called the hospital back and talked to the nurse again, and she was insulting. She accused me of not being the girl's father and how could she trust me to be who I said I was. I will tell you in this moment some of the most evil thoughts I ever had towards a person were happening. My mother was sitting next to me while all this was happening and could see what was happening in my mind. She looked at me and said Evan, don't tell me your daughter is one of those people. I responded, what do you mean? She said you know someone who is late even to their own funeral. In that very hard moment of my life it was humor from the spirit of God through my mother that helped me refocus versus wanting to plot evil towards this nurse. Long story short, that nurse never tried to locate my daughter's body and was dismissive of our situation the whole time. After I got someone else involved, they found our daughter still at the hospital. I ended up getting a fake lawyer "non-apology" letter from the hospital. I can't emphasize enough, how much humor got me out of a terrible place in that challenging moment – humor was from God. Do not be afraid to use humor. I believe God wants us to laugh, which is a fantastic form of medicine and healing.

"Matthew 4:5 NIV Blessed are those that mourn for they shall be comforted." Revelation 21:4 NIV 4 'He will wipe every tear from their eyes. There will be no more death or mourning or crying or pain, for the old order of things has passed away."

Global issues: These are a concern for many people. As the years go on and sin and lawlessness become more accepted, the state of the world can be soul-crushing. I like to remind people that God never made us carry the sins or weight of the world. That is his job, and that's why he sent Jesus. I tell people that our brains cannot handle the large source of negative news from all the corners of the earth. I encourage people to turn the news off and open their Bibles instead. I remind people that our faith and trust are in Jesus despite what we see going on in the world around us. Easier said than done, I know. But I remind people that we are not of this world but are here for only a short amount of time compared to eternity.

John 16:33 NIV 33: "I have told you these things, so that in me you may have peace. In this world, you will have trouble. But take heart! I have overcome the world." John 17:15 NIV 15 My prayer is not that you take them out of the world but that you protect them from the evil one.

CHAPTER 11

Living a Life of Influence

We all have influences in our lives. The way we think, the food we eat, and our interests. Regardless of how small, everything we are has been affected by outside influences. This can be a positive or negative experience. Look how Hollywood, music, and politics have been decaying our society. Most dominantly, it has not been healthy for us as a culture. This is where you and every Christian out there comes in. We might not have the reach of a celebrity, movie, music, or political pundit, but we do have influence. Regardless of your reach, you have influence. The best way to change the world is to change one person's life, because for that one person their world has changed. It is easy to fall into the trap of thinking that I am not influential, but I am hoping we can change that way of thinking. We can influence others even in our short interactions with them. We can influence the lives of those that we come into contact with.

How many times has a stranger done something that rubbed you the wrong way? That was an influence. We can influence people daily by how we live our lives and treat others around us. We can use these moments as God moments and see how God wants to invest in the lives of others that are a part of our daily routines. The most places of influence are on our families and friends. If you look at yourself as an influential person, you will see yourself as such. Influence is a central concept and key to many aspects of human life. It gives a person the ability to affect the thoughts, feelings, or actions of others in some way. Influence can be a force for good, or it can be a force for evil, and influence can come from various sources.

At its core, influence is about having an impact on the lives of others. So it can be as simple as persuading someone to see your point of view or as complex as influencing others into changing one's deeply held beliefs or values. It can be used for good or ill, and it can be wielded by anyone, regardless of status or position. Influence is a spiritual force designed by God to help us be transformed into his image in our desire to have a relationship with him. When God created influence, it was pure and sinless. Influence is also about free will. Without the ability to have influences, then we would not have choices. Without choices, we would not have free will.

God gave Adam and Eve the choice to be influenced by him or by the serpent, and they chose wrong. Influence is a way of bringing connection and identity into someone's life. **People often identify with what they are influenced by**. If you want to be helpful to others in your life and in service to the great commission, learn to influence. Communication is easily one of the most important aspects of influence. There are so many styles of communication that need to be considered when wanting to be influential. The use of language, the words we choose. The tonality in which we use and the way we frame or structure a talk or conversation.

The body language we use while communicating needs to be consistent with the message or conversation. Effective influence requires effective communication and understanding of the people or audiences' needs and beliefs. It also requires you to have empathy and emotional intelligence, as well as the ability to listen actively and respond thoughtfully. All of which we have in times of strife. But if you can be self-controlled, well thought out, and have the ability to speak and to listen to what is being said. It gives you better command, influence, and authority from which you can speak. 2 Timothy 1:17 For God has not given us a spirit of fear, but of power, love, and a sound mind. NIV

Credibility is another key element when it comes to being influential. The reason why we have news networks and celebrity endorsements is because, at some level, people trust them. Regardless of the fact, they are getting paid to do so. To be truly influential, a person must be perceived as trustworthy and credible by their captive audience. This requires a combination of expertise, experience, and integrity, as well as the ability to establish and maintain strong relationships with others or that you are a person who brings value into the lives of others. Influence has and will continue to come from many different sources. What are some of these other sources? Glad you asked. Some of the most common sources of influence include Authority, which refers to the office or power one may have over someone. This is when you must listen to someone because they have power or control in your life. Examples would be police, pastors, politicians, bosses, managers, teachers, and parents. Expertise refers to a person's knowledge and skills in a particular area that other people see and need. This would be an example of people like a doctor, firefighter, plumber, or lawyer. Charisma is when others want to watch, subscribe, and follow someone based on who they are and what they teach.

They are influential because they are both entertaining and they make people feel accepted. Their value is entertainment, or the ability to make people feel connected and good about themselves. They try to get people to believe they can have the life they have. Examples of this are social media influencers, public speakers, and ministers. Social proof is when someone has done something before and has built credibility or a reputation for doing it. An example is a home builder. They have built quality homes, Master gardeners, and great real estate agents. Charisma is kind of like the art of charm. It refers to the personal qualities that make a person more socially attractive and persuasive to others, such as confidence and enthusiasm. Social proof is when people have given you credibility, and because of this, it makes you more influential to others.

There are different types of influence. First is direct influence. Which involves actively persuading or convincing others to do something. This in evangelism is when you actively witness to someone about the Gospel. The second type of Influence is Indirect influence. An example of this would be a friendship over the years where your non-Christian friends are influenced by you simply because you are living out Christian principles. They see you have peace and want that in their own lives. This happens when you shape the environment so that it encourages or discourages certain behaviors or beliefs. I have been influenced many times by sermons or videos I have watched.

Influence is a spiritual force that is extremely powerful. It is a tool and can be used well or misused. It can help you reach personal goals. You can use it to motivate people, change attitudes, and drive action. It can be used in leadership to help encourage others to follow. If misused, either intentionally or unintentionally, it can be a force for manipulation towards personal gain or a tactic to make people do something in your best interest. Remember the garden and Adam and Eve. Influence done by God was leadership, offering free will and having a relationship with Him. The serpent used influence to push his will onto Adam and Eve to break the relationship between them and God because he was manipulating them to think that God was holding out on them.

Ultimately, the concept of influence is a complicated one that has been shaped by many different factors. Influence requires a level of understanding of human behavior, as well as the ability to communicate effectively, establish credibility, and build strong relationships with others.

What is lifestyle evangelism, and why does it matter? What is the concept of being a lifestyle evangelist as a way of life? My understanding and expression of the idea behind lifestyle evangelism is that it is a term used to describe how Christians should share the Gospel of Jesus Christ. This is about recognizing the opportunities that we have right in front of us every day to share the Gospel. This happens in the community and among the people with whom we live our life. This is about building relationships with people in the place you commonly frequent, as well as developing the skills to share the good news of Christ. As believers, we are being witnesses to Christ in the way in which we show up to the world around us by demonstrating His love, compassion, and grace in our daily interactions with others.

The idea behind lifestyle evangelism is that our actions and attitudes can have a profound impact on those around us and can lead others to inquire about our faith and the way we live, as well as the conversations in which we enter into with people around us. At the core of this concept, lifestyle evangelism is about living out the Great Commission (Matthew 28:19-20) in a way that is authentic and natural. It is not about imposing our beliefs on others but rather about sharing our faith in a way that is bold, respectful, loving, and non-judgmental. It is about building relationships with people, getting to know them, and showing them the love of Christ through our words and actions.

While some might think that the concept of being a lifestyle evangelist is new, it is not, and I wish I could take credit for that, but I can't. In fact, it is rooted in the teachings of Jesus Himself, who often used parables and stories to relate to people and the culture that would illustrate spiritual truths. Jesus did not just preach to the crowds; pack up and then go home. He spent time with individuals, showing them love, kindness, compassion, and grace. He demonstrated His love for people by healing the sick, feeding the hungry, and befriending the outcasts of society.

The Apostle Paul modeled lifestyle evangelism in his own life. He wrote in 1 Corinthians 9:19-23, "Though I am free and belong to no one, I have made myself a slave to everyone, to win as many as possible...I have become all things to all people so that by all possible means I might save some." Paul understood that effective evangelism requires a willingness to meet people where they are, to build relationships with them, and to share the Gospel in a way that is relevant to their lives. So why does lifestyle evangelism matter? There are several reasons:

1. It is a natural way to share the Gospel – Having done evangelism correctly and ineffective, I find many people are turned off by aggressive or confrontational evangelism tactics. While there is a time and place for confrontational evangelism, many people think this is the only way to do evangelism, but it is not. The most common way for people to evangelize will be operating in this Lifestyle evangelism which is a natural and non-threatening way to share our faith with others. By living out our faith in our daily lives and willing to introduce it to others as we go about our day. We can be a witness for Christ without being pushy or overbearing.

2. It is effective – Studies have shown people are more likely to be influenced by those they know and trust rather than by strangers or advertisements. By building relationships with people and demonstrating the love, power, and Authority of Christ, we can have a profound impact on their lives.

3. It is biblical – Jesus, the disciples, the Apostle Paul, and the church in Acts all modeled lifestyle evangelism in their own lives, and the Bible instructs us to be a witness for Christ in all areas of our lives. Acts 1:8 NIV But you will receive power when the Holy Spirit comes on you; and you will be my witnesses in Jerusalem, and in all Judea and Samaria, and to the ends of the earth." Jerusalem was a representation of the place where many of the people he was speaking to lived. The meaning is to be a witness in your own community. As Christians, we are called to be salt and light in the world, to shine the love and forgiveness of Christ in every situation. Some are called elsewhere, but most of us are called to be a witness where we are – wherever our feet are currently touching the ground.

4. Evangelism is inclusive – Lifestyle evangelism is not about excluding people who have a particular type of sin or overlooking someone who does not remotely share our beliefs. Lifestyle evangelism is about understanding the need to build relationships with all people, regardless of their sin, background, beliefs, or lifestyle. Jesus witnessed the people

who were caught in their sin, and when they met him, they were transformed. Evangelism is about showing others Christ and inviting all people to experience the love, hope, and joy that comes from a relationship with Him and that salvation through him brings.

5. It is a way of life. Jesus says in John 14: 6 "I am the way and the truth and the life. No one comes to the Father except through me. (NIV) While evangelism may have different techniques which may feel artificial, forced, or rehearsed, the idea and heart behind lifestyle evangelism is a way of life. It is integrating our faith in Jesus, sharing the salvation message in every area of our lives, and letting the love of Christ shine through in everything we do. As a human being myself, this is easier said than done. This is why it is important that we deny our flesh daily and follow Jesus. Without the discipline of laying our own ambitions down, people can feel like a distraction rather than a divine appointment and opportunity. Living a life of influence through the concept of lifestyle evangelism is a powerful and effective way to share with others the love of Jesus and the Gospel. Jesus says we are the light in Matthew 5:14-16

(NIV)14 "You are the light of the world. A town built on a hill cannot be hidden. 15 Neither do people light a lamp and put it under a bowl. Instead, they put it on its stand, and it gives light to everyone in the house. 16 In the same way, let your light shine before others, that they may see your good deeds and glorify your Father in heaven." Living as the light of the world through lifestyle evangelism is about living out our faith in a natural and authentic way so we can build relationships with people and demonstrate to them the love of Christ through our words and actions.

CHAPTER 12

Building Relationships
that Matter

In this thing called life, we find ourselves surrounded by people who are also doing life. We do life together with some people, and with others we keep our distance. Some relationships are short-term, and other relationships are life-long. Regardless of the relationship's longevity, it's important when building a relationship, we give it the attention the relationship warrants. I have relationships today that even though there is less connection with the person now than there was in the past, when a short reconnect happens, it's as if there was no distance or time between our last and present connection.

That's building relationships that matter. Regardless of time or distance, you are able to easily connect and reconnect with people that ebb and flow in and out of your life. I have seen people put up walls against people they had great relationships with in the past, simply because they are not as present in each other's lives. There is the idea that we have a limited amount of relational ability within ourselves. I come from the belief that I have the power of the living God in me, who has the ability to have a large variety of relationships. This does not mean your relationships are not structured and free for all. I am saying if you know the placement of that relationship in your life, then it is easier to expand your ability to relate and build relationships that matter.

Relationship structures

Some of the best examples of relationship structures are found by Jesus and Moses. When Jesus started his ministry, he called to himself twelve disciples. Peter, James, and John, the sons of Zebedee. Andrew, Philip, Thomas, Judas, Bartholomew, Matthew James, Simon the Zealot. Three of the twelve were closer to Jesus: Peter, James, and John. Out of the three, there was one closest to him, and that was self-proclaimed by John. The other followers of Jesus were not a part of the twelve., behind them were the people whom he ministered to and performed miracles for. Jesus had many relationships but at different levels of connection and intimacy.

Moses was trying to lead Israel as a one-person show. He would listen to all the disputes and try to be the judge as well as the leader. That was not working well. NIV Exodus 18:**17** Moses' father-in-law replied, "What you are doing is not good. **18** You and these people who come to you will only wear yourselves out. The work is too heavy for you; you cannot handle it alone. **19** Listen now to me, and I will give you some advice, and may God be with you. You must be the people's representative before God and bring their disputes to him. **20** Teach them his decrees and instructions and show them the way they are to live and how they are to behave. **21** But select capable men from all the people – men who fear God, trustworthy men who hate dishonest gain – and appoint them as officials over thousands, hundreds, fifties, and tens. **22** Have them serve as judges for the people at all times but have them bring every difficult case to you; the simple cases they can decide themselves. That will make your load lighter because they will share it with you. **23** If you do this and God so commands, you will be able to stand the strain, and all these people will go home satisfied."

Moses built a hierarchy of relationships. Not everyone deserves the same amount of attention. In Moses' closest Circle, God was first; then there was his brother Aaron and his sister Miriam. Behind them were Joshua and Caleb. Behind them it was the representatives. Behind them, it was all of Israel. When we build relationships that matter, it is important for us to know where to place people in our lives. Not everyone deserves a seat in the closest parts of our lives, but that does not mean they get ignored either. Jesus and Moses developing this structure could meet their call and still have a relational connection with the masses. Building connections and relationships is like creating fertile soil for the soul. This gives you the authority to speak the salvation message into people's lives.

How do we actually connect with other people?

Building relationships with people require us to be intentional about the investment of time and effort we put forth. In real estate, we had this saying that "if it's not on your calendar, it does not exist" in regard to lead generation. We prioritize people by making time in our lives for others. We put them into our calendar. What does this time look like? It could be a recreational sports team, a book club, golfing, getting a lunch, a coffee or even a phone call. When we spend quality time engaging in shared activities or being present in someone's life, we communicate to that person, people, or group that they have value, and thus, it reinforces the significance of the relationship. Jesus showed up in people's lives, and he performed miracles. He did not stay around long term. He was not afraid to show up in people's lives, even if he knew it was for a moment of time. This is where we redefine relationships. To most people, that would not be a relationship, but when you make a difference in someone's life, that is the premise for a relationship. I personally like to know what's going on in the lives of my friends. I want to be a good friend and a good witness. If someone is sick or had surgery, had a baby, or died, I want to send them a meal. If someone graduated or got a promotion, had a birthday, or hit a goal, I want to celebrate with them in person or by card or text.

When this type of relationship gets built, it becomes a pivotal evangelist role. When we can make meaningful connections, this enables us to display the love of Christ and build trust and authority while creating more opportunities for open dialogue about faith. Investing in people by focusing on relationships creates a solid foundation for effective and sustainable evangelism. Another way of being able to connect with people is by being authentic. Have you ever seen a speaker or met someone who just seems inauthentic? It's hard to minister to people if you are being fake. Authenticity is essential in building relationships that matter. I have found in my own life that being genuine and vulnerable allows others to see that I am not perfect, nor am I trying to pretend that I am. My imperfections, struggles, and growth are the very tools I use to create an environment of trust and relatability.

When we live out authenticity, it invites others to do the same, thus helping us to foster deeper connections and relationships. That then creates the opportunity for spiritual conversations and the opportunity to speak to the heart, the hurt, and the life of someone who needs Jesus – or just encouragement. One of my favorite content creators on social media is a man by the name of Gary Vaynerchuk. If you have sensitive ears, don't listen to him. While he is not a believer, he displays an amazing attribute for Empathy. This is an authentic trait of his. This is what attracts people to him. In addition to Empathy, he also shares hard truths, but in love. If he only had hard truths without Empathy, he probably would not be as successful. To first be able to listen creates the ability to be empathetic, which shows genuine interest in others. When other people feel you are interested in them, it moves you into the realm of being relatable. This, gives him a platform of authority which he uses to speak into people's lives; thus creating deeper and further connections and relationships. He exudes grace and compassion for other people, and because of this, people want to be around him.

We need to develop the attributes of Jesus because people want to be around those that have his attributes. I think of the "wee" little man named Zacchaeus and how his whole life was transformed because Jesus cared enough about him to have dinner at his house. Jesus bestowed the honor on him to be the host. Zacchaeus was an outcast, and the Jews did not like him but instead of Jesus criticizing him, he honored him, and in that honor, a man's heart was changed. When we live in love, joy, peace, patience, kindness, goodness, and self-control to others, we are showing them Jesus. When we embrace the cross, we change; when we live out the life of the cross, others change. Have you ever seen an act of kindness filmed and placed online? What about an act of kindness that ended up transforming someone's life? It is so encouraging to see videos of acts of kindness, but how much more glorifying to Christ, it is if we live life in a way that acts of kindness flow from our lives onto those that are around us.

I know this is something that I have to work towards and be aware of when I am living life. I have a son who is two and a half years old, and it's just a part of his nature. When I see him operate out of that gift to others and strangers, I see it impact them. When we live out the cross, and we have the chance to impact others through the power and timing of the holy spirit, God will touch people's lives regardless of the location you are at. I have seen this in restaurants, grocery stores, and many other places. When God is allowed to work through us because we are willing and we live in his nature, it leaves a profound impact on everywhere we go.

CHAPTER 13

Dealing with Fear

I am adding a chapter on fear because, as Christians, I have seen many of us struggle with it in our daily lives. Fear also is something that keeps us from living a lifestyle of evangelism. So, if I am going to address overcoming Fear in evangelism, I feel like I also need to include processing fear and anxiety in other areas of life. In some parts of this book, you have seen repeated themes. One of the repeated themes is overcoming one's Fear. Fear is an intricate and multifaceted emotion that has deep roots in the soul. In the mind, and through the evolutionary breakthroughs of science, we understand the brain in ways that we have never been able to in human history. Fear is a response to situations that create a behavior or outcome. What is the purpose of Fear?

From a neuroscience standpoint, Fear has helped humans see and process threats for survival throughout generations. It's the alert that scared me – made me jump out of my pants when I addressed a golf ball for my next shot and realized I had walked up on a rattlesnake only a foot away from my golf ball. [Side note: I was around 14 and my dad still made me get my golf ball.] The amygdala part of the brain is responsible for processing emotions, particularly fear, and plays a crucial role in this process. When our ancestors encountered potential threats like predators or dangerous situations, the amygdala would signal the body to prepare for action, whether it be to confront the danger or flee from it. Or, like me, run screaming like a little girl at a Justin Bieber concert.

What's the role of Fear in our lives today? While we may not face the same life-threatening dangers as our ancestors, our brains still respond similarly to perceived threats. Fear can be triggered by various factors, including traumatic experiences, phobias, social anxiety, and even learned behaviors throughout life. The brain's response to Fear is highly individual, as each person's past experiences, genetics, and environment shape their fear response.

When Fear becomes chronic or excessive, it can significantly negatively impact our physical and mental well-being. Prolonged exposure to stress hormones like cortisol can lead to health issues such as high blood pressure, weakened immune system, and sleep disturbances. Emotionally, Fear can contribute to anxiety disorders, depression, and avoidance behaviors that hinder our ability to live fulfilling lives. I have done a lot of studying on this subject because in 2021, it felt like it came out of nowhere. I was fighting constant panic attacks and daily anxiety. I first thought it was a heart attack. I am very sympathetic to people who struggle with Fear.

In a biblical context, Fear is a recurring theme addressed throughout the Scriptures. While the Bible acknowledges the reality of Fear, it consistently offers words of encouragement and comfort to those who seek God. Countless verses remind believers that God is with them, that they need not be afraid, and that He will provide strength and guidance in the face of Fear. For instance, Psalm 34:4 reassures us, "I sought the Lord, and He answered me; He delivered me from all my fears."

At the same time, the Bible also warns about the tactics of the enemy, Satan, who seeks to use Fear as a tool to keep us from living in the freedom and fullness of life that God intends for us. Satan can manipulate our fears and insecurities, planting doubt about God's love and goodness and undermining our faith and trust in God. In my journey of understanding and of processing Fear and anxiety, I found reflecting on my family history to be an eye-opening and transformative experience. I began to explore who else in my family might have dealt with similar issues and why they might have experienced it. Doing so gave me valuable insights into the root causes of my fears and anxieties.

Looking back, I realized that specific patterns and behaviors in my family might have contributed to developing my fears. It became clear that my environment and upbringing significantly shaped my emotional responses and coping mechanisms. Understanding the emotional climate I grew up in helped me recognize the origins of some of my fears and anxieties. As I looked into my past, I discovered recurring themes, such as the loss of close friends and being subjected to bullying for twelve years starting from a young age. These experiences profoundly impacted me, and I began to see how they shaped my perceptions and triggered my fears. Acknowledging these past events allowed me to confront the seeds of Fear that no longer serve a purpose in my life.

'Seeking guidance from multiple counselors and mentors has been invaluable on my healing journey. Fear goes beyond what is happening in the mind; **the mind is often the response to what is happening in the soul. Fear often stems from learned behavior, deep wounds, and generational patterns in the soul.** These wounds needed to be addressed to experience true healing and freedom.

My faith played a pivotal role in this process as well. By continually surrendering my fears and anxieties to God, I found relief and healing as I worked toward complete restoration. God desires to heal us holistically – spiritually, emotionally, mentally, and physically. By facing my Fear and anxiety, I am surrendering to God and allowing Him to work in my life. I have learned God won't address it unless I handle it. I can say a prayer for God to take my Fear away, but God won't do the work without me. I believe healing from the spirit of Fear is not just healing in my mind but also in my soul, body, and heart. This is a whole-person approach to healing and peace. This healing journey was not about dismissing the mind or the soul but recognizing that God's healing encompasses all aspects of who we are.

I have to laugh as I write this because I had a big anxiety attack the day I was to write about Fear and anxiety. Not because I was afraid of anything but because of genetic issues I am learning about and how I relate to digesting food. I am not perfect in the areas of rooting out all Fear and anxiety in my life, but I am much better at it now than I have been. I used to have major panic attacks that could last days. Now it's hours to only a few short minutes

When I confronted my fears, I experienced a sense of peace. I learned that true healing comes from acknowledging and addressing the root causes of our fears rather than simply masking the symptoms or asking God to take them away without any effort on my part. This reflective process enabled me to start breaking from generational patterns and embrace a new path of courage and trust in God's plan for my life.

Reflecting on family history and engaging in introspection can be instrumental in understanding and processing Fear and anxiety. By recognizing the origins of our fears and seeking holistic healing through God's grace, we can experience a transformative journey toward freedom and wholeness. Remember, you are fearfully and wonderfully made, and God desires to heal every aspect of your being. Embrace this healing journey and allow God's love and grace to lead you to a life of courage, faith, and peace.

CHAPTER 14

Understanding and Overcoming Fear: A Biblical and Neurological Perspective

From a biblical perspective, fear is a natural human response to perceived threats, but it can also become a tool used by the enemy to keep believers in bondage. Combining biblical insights with neuroscientific knowledge, we can gain a comprehensive understanding of fear, its impact on our bodies and nervous systems, and effective strategies to overcome it as Christians.

Overcoming Fear: A Biblical Approach:

1. Trusting in God's Promises: The Bible consistently encourages believers to trust in God's promises and seek His presence in times of fear. Verses like Isaiah 41:10 and Psalm 56:3 remind us that God is with us and that we need not be afraid. Cultivating a deeper relationship with God through prayer and studying His Word can strengthen our faith and alleviate fear.

2. Recognizing the Enemy's Tactics: By understanding that Satan uses fear as a tactic to keep us in bondage, we can stand firm in our faith and resist his attempts to manipulate our thoughts and emotions. Ephesians 6:10-12 reminds us to put on the armor of God, including the shield of faith, to protect ourselves from the enemy's attacks.

3. Casting Our Anxieties on God: The Bible encourages believers to cast their anxieties on God because He cares for them (1 Peter 5:7). When we surrender our fears to God, we acknowledge His sovereignty and trust that He is in control of our lives. This act of surrender can lead to a sense of peace and relief from the burden of fear.

4. Renewing Our Minds: Romans 12:2 urges us not to conform to the patterns of this world but to be transformed by the renewing of our minds. By focusing on God's truth and promises rather than dwelling on fear-inducing thoughts, we can rewire our thought patterns and cultivate a more positive and faith-centered mindset.

5. Practicing Gratitude and Worship: Philippians 4:6-7 advises believers to present their requests to God with thanksgiving. Engaging in a lifestyle of gratitude and worship shifts our focus from fear to God's goodness and faithfulness. As we praise and thank Him, fear's grip on our hearts weakens, allowing His peace to guard our minds.

IV. Overcoming Fear: A Neurological Approach:

1. Mindfulness and Breathing Techniques: Practicing mindfulness and deep breathing can activate the Peripheral

Nervous System (PNS) and help reduce the physiological effects of fear. Mindfulness involves being present at the moment and acknowledging our emotions without judgment. Deep breathing exercises promote more oxygen in your body and can calm the nervous system and promote relaxation.

2. Cognitive-Behavioral Techniques: Cognitive-behavioral therapy (CBT) is an evidence-based approach used to address fear and anxiety. It involves identifying and challenging negative thought patterns and replacing them with more rational and positive ones. CBT can rewire the brain's neural pathways, leading to lasting changes in behavior and emotional responses.

3. Exposure Therapy: Exposure therapy is a systematic approach to confronting fears and phobias in a controlled and safe environment. Gradually exposing oneself to fear-inducing stimuli can desensitize the brain's fear response, leading to decreased anxiety over time.

4. Physical Activity and Exercise: Regular physical activity and exercise release endorphins, the brain's natural mood enhancers, which can reduce stress and anxiety. Engaging in physical activity also diverts attention from fear-inducing thoughts and promotes a sense of well-being.

5. Seeking Professional Help: For individuals experiencing debilitating fear or anxiety, seeking professional help from therapists or counselors can be beneficial. These mental health professionals can provide personalized strategies and support tailored to each person's unique needs.

NOTE: This is one of the most beneficial things that I have found in my life to help me pre-plan my day and keep my mind and nervous system from tripping out on me. I have a small pop-up sauna, and a deep freezer converted into an ice bath.

6. Hot and cold exposure: Sauna and ice baths can be powerful tools in overcoming stress, anxiety, and fear. Saunas provide a relaxing environment that promotes physical and mental relaxation. The heat helps to soothe tense muscles, reduce cortisol levels, and release endorphins, the body's natural stress-relievers. This calming effect on the body can help alleviate anxiety and create a sense of peace and well-being. On the other hand, ice baths, also known as cold therapy, stimulate the release of norepinephrine, which can improve mood and cognitive function, helping to combat stress and fear. Additionally, the contrasting experience of going from the sauna's warmth to the ice bath's coldness can create a sense of resilience and mental toughness, empowering individuals to face their fears and challenges with a greater sense of control. The combination of heat and cold therapy in saunas and ice baths offers a holistic approach to reducing stress and anxiety, allowing individuals to find balance and restoration both physically and mentally. This is something I do a few times a week at home.

7. Incorporating intermittent fasting and weight loss into your self-care routine can have numerous benefits when it comes to overcoming fear and anxiety. Firstly, intermittent fasting has been shown to have positive effects on brain health and mental well-being. During fasting periods, the body produces ketones, which can provide a source of energy for the brain and may help improve cognitive function and mood regulation. This can lead to reduced anxiety and a greater sense of mental clarity and focus. Intermittent fasting can also promote emotional resilience. By intentionally abstaining from food for certain periods, you practice self-discipline and develop a sense of control over your body and mind. This newfound discipline can translate into other areas of your life, including how you cope with fear and anxiety. It empowers you to face challenges with greater confidence and adaptability.

When it comes to weight loss, shedding excess pounds can boost your overall well-being and self-esteem. Physical activity and a balanced diet release endorphins, which are natural mood elevators. Regular exercise can help reduce stress and anxiety by promoting the release of neurotransmitters that induce relaxation and happiness. Feeling more confident about your body and health can also enhance your self-image and reduce self-doubt and fear. Additionally, a healthy body and mind are interconnected. As you take care of your physical health through intermittent fasting and weight loss, your mental health can also benefit. A healthier body can lead to improved sleep patterns, increased energy levels, and better overall emotional regulation, all of which contribute to a more positive outlook and greater resilience in the face of fear and anxiety.

Remember, self-care is not just about pampering yourself; it's about taking intentional steps to nurture your mind, body, and soul. Intermittent fasting and weight loss can be powerful components of a comprehensive self-care routine that empowers you to face fear and anxiety head-on, fostering a sense of empowerment and well-being in your daily life. Always consult with a healthcare professional before starting any new diet or exercise regimen to ensure it aligns with your individual needs and health goals.

To overcome the fear of witnessing to others, we can implement five biblical strategies that empower and embolden us to share our faith with confidence and love:

1. Prayer and Trust: Prayer is our direct line of communication with God, and through it, we seek His guidance and strength for the task of witnessing. We ask the Holy Spirit to empower us with courage and wisdom as we share the gospel with others. Trusting in God's faithfulness and knowing that He equips us for this mission, we approach witnessing with a firm belief that He will work through us.

2. Focus on Love: Witnessing is not about judgment or condemnation but an act of sharing God's love and grace with others. By emphasizing the love of God in our conversations, we convey genuine care and compassion for those we speak to. Understanding that each person is on their own journey, we approach discussions with open hearts and seek to understand their perspectives, fostering meaningful connections.

3. Study God's Word: To effectively share the gospel, we need a strong foundation in God's Word. Regularly immersing ourselves in the Scriptures allows us to internalize God's promises and truths. The more familiar we become with the Bible, the more confidence we gain in sharing its life-transforming message with others.

4. <u>Start Small</u>: Taking the first step in witnessing can be intimidating, so it's helpful, to begin with close friends or family members who are open to spiritual conversations. As we gain experience and grow in confidence, we can gradually extend our outreach to others beyond our immediate circle. Starting small allows us to refine our approach and build momentum in sharing our faith.

5. <u>Community Support</u>: Being part of a supportive Christian community can be a great source of encouragement and strength in our evangelistic efforts. Surrounding ourselves with like-minded friends who share a passion for evangelism provides a space to share experiences, seek advice, and pray for one another. Together, we uplift and motivate each other to be courageous witnesses for Christ.

By implementing these biblical strategies, we can overcome fear and step into a fulfilling role of sharing the life-changing message of the gospel. With prayer, love, knowledge of God's Word, starting small, and the support of a faith-filled community, we can confidently engage in witnessing, knowing that God is at work in and through us to touch hearts and bring others into a deeper relationship with Him. Overcoming the fear of rejection is a transformative journey that can be enriched by applying five biblical principles. These principles have resonated with me deeply, especially in this personal story of how I conquered the fear of rejection through faith and God's grace.

Growing up, I often struggled with feeling accepted and valued by my peers. Rejection seemed to lurk around every corner, leaving me feeling insecure and unworthy. As

I embarked on my journey of faith, I learned my true identity lies in Christ alone. I discovered that God's love for me is unwavering, regardless of what others might think or say. Renewing my mind became a pivotal step in conquering my fear of rejection. Just because I overcame it does not mean that I don't face its temptations. I started meditating on God's truth and promises daily – instead of dwelling on negative thoughts, I focused on things that were true, noble, and praiseworthy. As I anchored my thoughts in God's Word, my mind was gradually transformed, and the grip of fear began to loosen.

Embracing rejection as a possibility was a tough but necessary lesson for me. I realized that even Jesus faced rejection during His ministry on Earth. Understanding that rejection is a natural part of life allowed me to free myself from the burden of seeking constant approval from others. I grew bolder in sharing my faith, knowing that my worth was not determined by people's responses. And forgiveness played a crucial role in my journey of overcoming rejection. I carried wounds from past experiences of rejection, and bitterness that had taken root in my heart. However, as I delved deeper into my faith, I recognized the power of forgiveness in releasing that burden. I forgave those who had hurt me, and in doing so, I found healing and restoration in God's love.

Trusting in God to be my anchor during moments of potential rejection, I surrendered control and placed my trust in God's plan, I found peace and comfort. I held onto the promise that God works all things for the good of those who love Him, and even in moments of rejection, He was molding me for His greater purposes.

Through the integration of neuroscience and biblical principles, I not only understood the roots of my fear but also experienced the freedom to embrace my true identity in Christ. This journey of overcoming rejection strengthened my faith, emboldened me to share God's love with others fearlessly, and allowed me to live authentically as the person God created me to be. With God's love and these biblical principles, I no longer allowed fear of rejection to hold me back. Instead, I stepped into a life of purpose, driven by faith and unshaken by the opinions of others.

Conclusion

Understanding and overcoming fear from both biblical and neurological perspectives is a holistic and empowering process. Acknowledging the spiritual battle behind fear, trusting in God's promises, and cultivating a faith-centered mindset are essential for believers to live in freedom and overcome fear's hold on their lives. Simultaneously, applying neuroscientific knowledge and evidence-based strategies can empower individuals to address fear on a neurological level, promoting mental and emotional well-being. By integrating biblical principles and neurological insights, Christians can journey towards fearlessness, embracing God's call to live in courage and love.

Printed in the USA
CPSIA information can be obtained
at www.ICGtesting.com
LVHW020900100724
784894LV00005B/19